Whether you are a seasoned leader or just embarking on your leadership journey, this book provides insights that will resonate with women from all walks of life. I recommend this book to all who seek a richer experience and understanding of the links between God's providence and peoples' search for richer lives.

Allison Jackson, President, Allison Jackson Associates, LLC, Author and Speaker, Ringoes, New Jersey

Kim Dudley's chapter beautifully navigates the intersection of faith and the professional world. The author profoundly weaves practical advice with spiritual insight, guiding readers on how to infuse God and spirituality into their workplace journey. A truly inspiring read that not only imparts valuable insights but also encourages a transformative approach to the professional landscape.

Candice Grose, Deputy Chief of Communications, Cleveland Metropolitan School District, Cleveland, Ohio

Rev. Yolanda Jackson is indeed a woman of God, a woman of faith, and a woman of survival. She has strong faith, and it's evident in this book. Discover her relationship with God and how she resonates with a woman of substance, Mary Magdalene. Rev. Yolanda has empowered women who are called and struggling with the importance and significance of answering that call. Her story is of someone who has been rejected, downcast, lowly in heart, and oppressed, but through it all demonstrates faith and the importance of maintaining a relationship with God and forgiving others, moving forward and onward to a higher and better relationship and purpose in this world. This book will surely set you free to be who you are, and it will help you understand what God is calling you to do.

Rev. Dr. Patricia A. Wilson-Cone, ACPE Certified Educator, Senior Pastor, First American Baptist Church, Anchorage, AK

This book is a must read! I found myself immersed in the awesome testimonies, and as I read each chapter, I was reminded of how great and mighty God is. I enjoyed how the authors seamlessly wove scripture and Christian principles into their stories. Kim's chapter demonstrates how to rely on God. How He responds to her proves that all things are possible with God in our personal life and professional careers. This book will bless all who read it. It certainly blessed me!

Daphne L. Williams, People Leader, Enterprise Learning Office, Las Vegas, Nevada

Rev. Deleesa Meashintubby's journey from a girl growing up in Huntington, Arkansas to an accomplished businesswoman intrigues me. As I have watched her over the years, she has given me the heart to know that we are all called to a higher level of help to those around us.

Anissa Meashintubby, Eugene Oregon

As a highly respected business leader, Lisa Marchetti is known for her faith-based approach to overcoming diversity. She boldly shares her faith in Christ and undeterred commitment to His leading. Even when Lisa's strength could have suffered when her son and husband's cancer were diagnosed within the same year, Lisa drew her strength from God's living Word— faith anchored in scripture. Today Lisa is a testament to God's faithfulness in all aspects of life. Thank you, Lisa for boldly sharing your personal relationship with Jesus and the power of His unlimited love.

Valerie Sokolosky, Leadership Developing Trainer, Coach, and Author, Dallas, Texas

Women Leading By Faith:

Making a Difference NOW!

Compiled by

**Dr. Amanda H. Goodson
and Dr. Yvette Rice**

Women Leading By Faith: Making a Difference NOW!
Compiled by Dr. Amanda H. Goodson and Dr. Yvette Rice
Featured authors (in alphabetical order): Edith Brown (Foreword), Kim Dudley, Dr. Amanda Goodson, Je're Harmon, Rev. Yolanda Jackson, Elisa Marchetti (Lisa), Rev. DeLeesa Meashintubby, Dr. Yvette Rice, Odetta Scott, Dr. Nannette Wright

Editing: Adam Colwell's WriteWorks, LLC, Adam Colwell and Ginger Colwell
Book Design: To be added by Amanda
Published by Amanda Goodson Global, LLC

Printed in the United States of America
ISBN (Paperback): $19.99 / 978-1-951501-39-6
ISBN (eBook): $12.99 / 978-1-951501-40-2

The following Bible translations are used as follows, in order of their first appearance. Scriptures marked NLT are taken from the HOLY BIBLE, NEW LIVING TRANSLATION, Copyright© 1996, 2004, 2007 by Tyndale House Foundation. Used by permission of Tyndale House Publishers, Inc., Carol Stream, Illinois 60188. All rights reserved. Scriptures marked NIV are taken from THE HOLY BIBLE, NEW INTERNATIONAL VERSION®. Copyright© 1973, 1978, 1984, 2011 by Biblica, Inc.™. Used by permission of Zondervan. Scriptures marked NKJV are taken from the NEW KING JAMES VERSION®. Copyright© 1982 by Thomas Nelson, Inc. Used by permission. All rights reserved. Scriptures marked KJV are taken from the KING JAMES VERSION, public domain. Scriptures marked AMP and AMPC are taken from the AMPLIFIED® BIBLE, Copyright © 1954, 1958, 1962, 1964, 1965, 1987 by the Lockman Foundation Used by Permission.

While the authors have made every effort to provide accurate internet addresses at the time of publication, neither the publisher nor the authors assume any responsibility for errors or for changes that occur after publication. Further, the publisher does not have any control over and does not assume any responsibility for author or third-party websites or their content.

Acknowledgements

Kim Dudley

Thank you, God, for your daily grace and mercies and for pouring into me so that I can pour into others. Special thanks to my best friend and the love of my life, my husband, Steven Dudley, for his unwavering love, support, and encouragement. To my two children, Dr. Steven Dudley, Jr. and Sydney Dudley, thank you for knowing how and when to show up and for always giving your best efforts. Thank you, Dr. Goodson, for the opportunity to be part of one of your many great, God-given visions. I dedicate my chapter to my mother and father, Cora and Harvey Lewis.

Dr. Amanda H. Goodson

I'd like to thank my family for their continued support in my endeavors to write, speak, train, and coach along with so many other things that I have the opportunity to be blessed to do. To my husband, Lonnie, you are such an amazing man, and you are perfect for me. To my son, Jelonni, thank you for loving me how I am and for allowing me to love you back. To my mom, sister, and extended family, thank you so very much for always being there for me.

Je're Harmon

Thank you to my wonderful mentor, Dr. Amanda Goodson, for inviting me to be a part of this wonderful project and for your continued support and encouragement. To my parents, Marlon and Lisa Harmon, and other family and friends, thank you for your love and support throughout my life.

Rev. Yolanda Jackson

God blessed me to be part of a wonderful group of co-authors, and I was honored to have been asked to support this amazing project. Special thanks to my family, friends, and mentors who continue to inspire me to live my purpose!

Elisa Marchetti (Lisa)

Thank you, Dr. Amanda H. Goodson, for bringing to life this vision of different perspectives and expertise to show how women in the Bible and our current fellow sisters in Christ can continue to minister to us today. I am deeply appreciative for each of the co-authors and consider it a joy and honor to be part of this incredible work. Special thanks to my husband, Alex, and son, Sal, who display God's gifts of strength, perseverance, and hope in our lives. Lastly, I am incredibly grateful to my parents, Pastor Dan and Kathy Rohlwing, who encouraged me to never stop studying the Word of God.

Rev. DeLeesa Meashintubby

I am honored to be part of a wonderful group of co-authors, and I was blessed to have been asked to support this amazing project. Special thanks to my wonderful family and my talented mentors, whom I also consider my friends, who continue to pave the way and inspire me and others to live our purpose.

Dr. Yvette Rice

I give God all the glory and honor, for I could do nothing without Him. I extend a loving thank you to my husband, Bishop Sam Rice, Th.D.; our children, Sharné and Christopher; and our daughter-in-law, Amber; for their patience, encouragement, and support. Thank you to my parents, the late Maurice and Annie Harris; and my sister, Gloria Flowers, for believing I could go forth as a gospel minister, entrepreneur, and author. Thank you to the New Genesis Community Church family for their prayers. Thank you, Dr. Amanda H. Goodson and the other authors of this book, who have poured their hearts out to enlighten other women with dreams and vision and let them know that faith is their value proposition.

Odetta Scott

A sincere thank you to my husband, parents, family, and friends. Having you in my corner to provide support has proved invaluable. Thank you to all of my mentors who have poured into me and to my mentees who have allowed me to pour into them. Each one reach one!

Dr. Nannette Wright

Thank you, Holy Spirit, for guiding me on what to say and connecting me with all of these wonderful authors. To my loving husband, son, family, and friends, thank you for always praying for me and encouraging me. Iron sharpens iron, and I am forever grateful for sharpening you and the ways you have sharpened me.

Table of Contents

Foreword

Be Your Authentic Self

Edith Brown

Founder and CEO of Brown Coaching and Consulting

When I received my calling to live out my faith in God in the marketplace in 1987, I wish this book had been available. It provides the validation and inspiration that I couldn't find back then. As a former technology officer at Collins Aerospace and a Fortune 200 executive for the last 35-plus years, it often felt very lonely showing up in my marketplace as a woman of faith—and the community of women found here in *Women Leading by Faith: Making a Difference NOW!* encourages my heart as they highlight the freedom their faith has given them in their careers and personal lives.

In his book, *Every Good Endeavor,* author Timothy Keller speculates that, if Christians began to work as if they were serving the Lord, they would be free from both overwork and underwork. Money and acclaim would not be their controlling considerations because their work would become a way to please God by doing His work in the world. That's incredible—and it communicates exactly how the women in this book, who are so confident and qualified in so many areas, see their work. To them it is primarily a way to please God and connect their faith to what He has called them to do in their unique marketplace settings. They work and live in the freedom their faith has given them!

I most admire how each of the writers in *Women Leading by Faith: Making a Difference NOW!* displays such humble confidence in their various roles. They do an excellent job explaining how we can appreciate and enjoy our work while honoring God and serving others. They share their triumphs and successes as well as their failures and defeats. Whether it was, "I felt like I was betrayed," or "I felt like someone else got the credit for the work that I was doing," they were always able to reframe their experiences around God getting the glory.

I also loved their use of biblical women and how they brought the theology of each of those women into their own stories in such a rich way. The Bible verse that resonated with me as I engaged in their stories was Colossians 3:17. "Whatever you do or say, do it as a representative of the Lord Jesus, giving thanks through him to God the Father." (NLT) *Women Leading by Faith: Making a Difference NOW!* shows how God has always used women to impact the lives of others, bring glory to Him, and achieve His purposes. This is a powerful truth for the season we are in right now as a nation.

All of us want to find meaning in our work. These women, with very different vocational paths, found a way to build careers with purpose, and they truly make a profound impact on how our world is nourished. They walk by faith and exemplify their values to have a significant impact in the marketplace, balancing their family lives and their call to ministry with their work while highlighting the gifts of wisdom, leadership, compassion, health, discernment, preaching, and teaching. The Holy Spirit was with them every step of the way.

My mission today is to help leaders deliver with excellence and show up as themselves. As I stated earlier, when I first started in corporate America, it was very lonely. There was a tremendous amount of pressure on me to assimilate and be like everyone else. As a woman of faith, I knew I could not do that. I could not be like everybody else, yet I felt called to corporate America. It was very important to me to be Edith, my authentic self. I couldn't show up at work and *not* be a woman of faith.

That is the catalyst for my coaching and consulting business—and the same enduring theme of professional and personal authenticity flows throughout *Women Leading by Faith: Making a Difference NOW!* As you read the stories of the women in this book, they will inspire you. They will encourage you. They will convict you. They will motivate you to be your authentic self and live your best life because your work truly matters to God!

Introduction

On the Shoulders of Giants

Dr. Amanda H. Goodson and Dr. Yvette Rice

*A*s women of faith in the marketplace, we understand the importance of our trust in God as we fulfill the destinies, purposes, and plans that He has given us. Therefore, it is no surprise that we are inspired by the many strong women in the Bible who made an incredible difference in their various "marketplaces" of influence. Their stories equip and empower us through times of difficulty or when our faith is tested—and they will do the same for you as a business owner, someone who is pursuing your career working for someone else, or someone who aspires to get there. As we overcome the obstacles before us, we truly do so by the word of our testimonies!

That's why *Women Leading By Faith: Making a Difference NOW!* will inspire you. It features our stories, along with those from seven other incredible women, who are standing on the shoulders of the giants who came before us—the biblical women whose testimonies bring out the uniqueness and color they brought to the table to infuse our lives today.

We purposefully chose women for *Women Leading By Faith: Making a Difference NOW!* who are entrepreneurs. These women have been in the marketplace and understand it, and they appreciate the demands on them and their gifts. We asked these articulate, strong, savvy, and smart women, who are navigating it all while still being soft, faithful, loving, kind, gracious, and tenacious in everything they do, to speak up, tell their story, and intertwine it with the woman from the Bible who most informs their own faith in the marketplace. Who is it from Scripture who helps them be the person God called them to be right now so that they can love and fulfill the life God has called them to live as leaders?

Odetta Scott uses Sarah, the mother of the Hebrew nation, God's chosen people who received His covenant promise of love and salvation, to deliver her keen observations on how you can follow His plan, not yours.

Dr. Amanda H. Goodson gleans from the life of Leah in Genesis 29-33, a woman that almost everybody had counted out and certainly someone no one thought could achieve the extraordinary, to show you how the impossible is indeed possible for you.

Elisa Marchetti (Lisa) journeys back in time to the life of Deborah in Judges 4-5 to discern five characteristics of her life, what she calls the "Five C's of Faith," that are relevant for you today as you seek to exemplify your faith in the marketplace where you serve.

Je're Harmon teaches out of the extraordinary Old Testament story of Ruth to let you know how you can respond to your life's circumstances so that every single thing belongs to Him.

Dr. Nannette Wright dives into the dynamic life of Esther in the Old Testament to share her thoughts and encouragements so that you can let His light shine through you.

Kim Dudley features Mary, the mother of Jesus, and describes how she persevered and pressed forward to advance the Kingdom of God in her society with unwavering faith so that you can do the same.

Rev. Yolanda Jackson draws from the incredible life of Mary Magdalene, the first person to see Jesus after He rose from the dead, to exhort you to practice your faith in God with unwavering belief.

Rev. DeLeesa Meashintubby introduces you to the New Testament merchant Lydia to provide lessons and insights on how you can have a life of giving back and giving hope.

Dr. Yvette Rice takes you to the book of Acts and the impactful life of Priscilla to show you how to keep moving the mountains you face at work and at home as a woman of faith.

In each chapter, each author vulnerably, poignantly, and sometimes humorously reveals events from their own lives where they put what they learned from these giants of the Christian faith into practice in their own lives to help you discover how you can apply them to yours.

Not surprisingly, all of the women featured in this book are just like you—facing many of the challenges, prejudgments, and gender inequities those great women of the Bible experienced. Did you realize, for example, that it took until the Women's Business Ownership Act of 1988 for women to be able to get a business loan in the United States without the requirement of a male cosigner? Even with that long overdue breakthrough, women still routinely earn far less than men for the same job or position. That doesn't even speak to the systemic or unspoken bias women face in today's marketplace culture.

Yet here's the truth: you can operate in the marketplace and know that it is okay for you to be who you are and like you are right now! It is desirable for you to leverage the Word of God and allow it to permeate every fiber of your being, so you can become the woman of faith God called you to be and to *live it out* in your marketplace!

There are three reasons for this. First, God has given you favor. In Genesis 1:27-28, it says, "So God created mankind in his own image, in the image of God he created them; male and female he created them. God blessed them and said to them, 'Be fruitful and increase in number; fill the earth and subdue it. Rule over the fish in the sea and the birds in the sky and over every living creature that moves on the ground.'" (NIV) This was His blessing. It is His imperative.

Second, God has made you a bringer of life. Isaiah 54:1-2 declares, "'Sing, barren woman, you who never bore a child; burst into song, shout for joy, you who were never in labor; because more are the children of the desolate woman than of her who has a husband,' says the Lord. 'Enlarge the place of your tent, stretch your tent curtains wide, do not hold back; lengthen your cords, strengthen your stakes.'" (NIV)

Third, God has created you to shine! Isaiah 54:11-12 proclaims, "Afflicted city, lashed by storms and not comforted, I will rebuild you with stones of turquoise, your foundations with lapis lazuli. I will make your battlements of rubies, your gates of sparkling jewels, and all your walls of precious stones." (NIV)

Some women in the marketplace haven't had an opportunity to operate in that favor, bring life to expand themselves, or shine as brightly as they can. Yet we serve a mighty God who gives us *purpose* and a place of *presence*. We are to be God's gems in our areas of influence, glistening as precious stones through our leadership character and qualities. Just as a diamond has varying facets—windows cut into a stone that refract light and create gorgeous optical effects that make the diamond sparkle—we bring different strengths that allow us to bring unspeakable beauty and excellence to all that we do in the marketplace.

So, be encouraged, woman of God! You are right where you need to be, you are right on time, and you are doing the right thing, even though you may think you still have a ways to go. It's all part of the growth process. You are not done developing! Tie those bootstraps, keep moving, and continue rolling toward becoming and being the person God has called you to be. Beyond any shadow of a doubt, you are beautiful just as you are!

Like the bud of a flower, as you open and blossom the glory of God is being revealed! You are going to be so pleased when you look back on yourself five or ten years from now and *behold* what you have become. Just as the women of the Bible have touched and inspired us, you will be the woman—the giant who comes before them—to touch and inspire others.

Stand tall and shine bright! You are a part of the tapestry of generational excellence as a woman of faith in the marketplace.

Selah.

1

His Plan, Not Yours

Odetta Scott

Sarah

"Is anything too hard for the Lord? I will return about this time next year, and Sarah will have a son."

(Genesis 18:14, NIV)

I am not afraid to be my authentic self in how I walk, talk, and treat those around me. My desire is to be an example to others, so they become curious and ask why I am the way I am.

Expressing my faith in the marketplace translates to my ability to live my beliefs both internally and externally.

That means encouraging those in need, connecting with others who believe, and engaging those who don't. Really, it is all about meeting people where they are. That draws others to God.

What I do in the morning sets me up for success. I get up early and read the Word, study, meditate, and pray. Then I go to the gym to work out and build the strength of my body, my external temple. At the end of the workout, our class prays as a group. We gather in the center of the room and invite those who are interested to join us in a circle. We hold hands, ask if there are any prayer requests for those who might have specific needs, then an individual prays for the entire group. That is very unique, and it's one of the reasons I enjoy my workout so much. We initially started with about three people out of the 10 or so who participate in the workout, but that has increased to up to seven people praying with us. We are a family, standing in the gap and exercising our faith to meet the challenges we face each day and to help others get through the hard times they encounter. That builds up my spirit, my internal temple.

While the Bible is filled with many inspiring women of faith, Sarai, who was later renamed Sarah, is the woman I most admire. She was the mother of the Hebrew nation, God's chosen people who received His covenant promise of love and salvation. More than that, she wasn't perfect. She had genuine, human flaws. But she was later noted in Scripture for her strong yet submissive faith (Hebrews 11:11, 1 Peter 3:6).

Her husband, Abram, was first told by God that his descendants would be as numerous as the stars in the sky (Genesis 15:5). Problem was, Sarai was barren. She could not have children. So, in desperation to become a mother, and frustrated that God had restrained her from bearing children (Genesis 16:2), she gave her personal servant, Hagar, to her husband as a concubine. Though Hagar became pregnant and had a son, Ishmael, for Abram, Sarai despised Hagar. Her presumptive actions also did nothing to quench her longing to be a mother. Sarai was not practicing the kind of faith that comes "by hearing, and hearing by the word of God." (Romans 10:17, NKJV).

In Genesis 17, God appeared to Abram, changed his name to Abraham, and reiterated His earlier declaration, saying that Abraham would become a father of many nations (Genesis 17:5). God also told him that Sarai, now to be called Sarah, would have a son and be "the mother of nations; kings of peoples shall be from her." (Genesis 17:16, NKJV) However, Sarah did not learn of this promise herself until three men that Bible scholars speculate were angels, or possibly even manifestations of the godhead (Father, Son, and Holy Spirit), visited her husband. One of them made an incredible announcement. "And He said, 'I will certainly return to you according to the time of life, and behold, Sarah your wife shall have a son.' (Sarah was listening in the tent door which was behind him.) Now Abraham and Sarah were old, well advanced in age; and Sarah had passed the age of childbearing. Therefore Sarah laughed within herself, saying, 'After I have grown old, shall I have pleasure, my lord being old also?'" (Genesis 18:10-12, NKJV)

It was an amazing declaration, one that Sarah clearly had trouble believing. I love her humanity. Ultimately, though, God kept His promise, and Sarah did conceive and gave birth to a son, Isaac, who became a direct ancestor of Jesus Christ. "And Sarah said, 'God has made me laugh, and all who hear will laugh with me.' She also said, 'Who would have said to Abraham that Sarah would nurse children? For I have borne him a son in his old age.'" (Genesis 21:6-7, NKJV)

Sarah's story teaches me that God doesn't need our help. He wants us to be faithful to Him. We have to know the Word and keep it in our heart. It also shows me that I can't get caught up in what I see. As of this writing, in the summer of 2023, I was in a particular season where I had to remain faithful and know that my next opportunity for growth was coming. It seemed like it was taking a long time, longer than I would've liked. I had to remind myself to walk in faith, not by sight (2 Corinthians 5:7)—and I still do. I am a King's kid, and whatever comes next will occur in His timing, not mine.

Perhaps you can relate. Such seasons are very challenging and confusing, just as Sarai could not comprehend how the Lord was going to bless her with a child when she was old. Yet I know that as we trust in God and wait on Him, our blessing will come, and it will be incredible and bring glory to Him.

When I started working for the Fortune 500 company I work for today, I was bitten by the process improvement bug, so much so that I was determined to get a Six Sigma Black Belt certification. Six Sigma is a widely used set of techniques and tools for process improvement. Getting my certification was going to require some training, after which I would identify a project that I could lead, and then present the project, my journey, and the results to a panel of company vice presidents.

Over a six month period, I diligently learned, selected and carried out a project, and prepared my presentation. I walked into the room where the leaders sat on one side of the table, like an evaluation board, and I was on the other. As though the situation was not already intimidating enough, that meeting setup did not help. I then gave my presentation—only to be informed by the panel that I had not earned my certification. I was emotionally distraught, and I'm sure the disappointment was obvious in my facial expression. I don't have a very good poker face. *What did I do incorrectly?* I lamented. *Why did this happen?*

Yet after hearing the panel's feedback, I understood. I had mistakenly presented a project where I owned only a portion of it. My presentation was also too broad, covering more than just my sliver of the work and its outcomes. I worked diligently to come up with a different project, and I spent countless hours making sure that I owned it. I knew it backward and forward and anticipated the questions they would ask. I learned from my failure—and nine months later, I presented my second project. The vice presidents questioned me, and I answered them based on the activities I completed.

They offered recommendations for potential next steps, then they paid me the greatest compliment.

"You are an energized change agent. Certification granted."

Over my career, I've had several other interactions with leaders that weren't so positive. Each one, however, challenged me in my skill set, which helped me to grow. When I was going through the circumstances, it was difficult to see that. Only when I was through the valley and on the other side did I see the growth I had experienced. In one situation, I worked for a program director whose leadership style was very different from mine. The program itself was woefully behind in overall metrics, particularly with the budget. While I could not stop the bleeding, I knew I could help turn the ink from red to pink.

As work on the project escalated, I found myself at a point where I had to have a very difficult conversation with the program director in order to gain alignment on how we were going to direct the team to meet our deliverables. In the meeting, I clearly articulated my perspective on the situation as the engineering lead. I stated that he and I had to get in alignment on the directives being provided to the team. Specifically, I wanted him to communicate with me first before he sent one of my engineers off on a different task. "We have to work collaboratively to drive the team in the right direction," I said. "They need to see us working together to achieve program performance, not battling against one another. It's our job to remove road-blocks for the team, not create them."

He listened, then replied, "Yes, our styles are very different," he told me, "and I actually requested for you to be on this team. We need your leadership style to help collaborate and drive better solutions."

I was taken aback. I didn't think he knew the value that I brought to the team, much less recognized it, but clearly, he did. It was a reminder that our assumptions are often incorrect. In fact, when I am escalated emotionally, I tend to place a totally different narrative on the issue based on my assumptions. Six months after starting the work, and at the end of the year, he gave me a monetary reward for the results and leadership I provided.

In this and all other situations I face in the market-place, faith serves as my internal compass. My constant prayer is that I will be led by my faith and stay on the path God has ordained for me. I ask the Lord to minimize me and maximize Himself so that others might be drawn to

Him. In response to that prayer, He consistently provides opportunities for me to share my faith. When I first came to work for my current employer, my boss had recently lost her mother. She was mad at God and disengaged so much she said she no longer believed. Her personal faith was shattered. The Lord used my relationship with her, and my belief and relationship with Him, to bring her back to Him. It was humbling and fulfilling!

As a professional, I aspire to be an executive at some point in my career. My thought behind that is the higher up I go in an organization, the more people I can help. I can make a larger impact for Him and His Kingdom. But I need to understand and seek Him for guidance. Is this what He has for me? Does this allow His plan to go forth? As I ask those questions, I ensure that my desire to progress up the corporate ladder is not in conflict with my faith or sense of contentment. "I have learned in whatever state I am, to be content," the Apostle Paul teaches in Philippians 4:11-13. "I know how to be abased, and I know how to abound. Everywhere and in all things I have learned both to be full and to be hungry, both to abound and to suffer need. I can do all things through Christ who strengthens me." (NKJV)

I have also learned to remember that God is always working in the background on my behalf, even though I may not see it. For example, when I did not obtain my Six Sigma certification the first time out, I was very disappointed, and I had to reflect and seek to understand what happened and why. By reframing the situation, looking at it from a different perspective, I discovered what I needed to correct. As I started over with a new project, God used the learning process to fuel me to correct my course and obtain the certification. Everything happened the way it did for a reason. God was at work in my life behind the scenes. Trust that the same is true for you in whatever setback you may be facing right now. You may not understand it when you are going through the storm or the valley, but when you get to the other side, you can connect the dots, see why it happened that way, and recognize what God was doing along the way in your life.

There was a situation in my career where some of my coworkers betrayed me and did not treat me well. As I reframed that circumstance, I stood my ground for who I was, but I did not treat them the same way they treated me. I didn't retaliate or stoop to their level. I took the high road. God helped me to keep my head up, knowing that what He has for me is *for* me, and no one can take that away. He has ordained it. I am not perfect by any means. I am still a work in progress—but it is my desire to walk in integrity full-time, 365 days a year. I understand that I am ultimately accountable to God. His expectation is that I will walk in integrity, regardless of the actions of others.

As much as it is in my ability to do so, I remain humble. I don't assume credit for myself. I always want to help others get recognition. I believe this so much that I have a saying that I try to live by every day to encourage and help others: "Each one reach one." When I was a preadolescent, I decided I wanted to be an astronaut. Something about the uniqueness of the career, the hard work it would take to attain it, and the reward it would bring excited me. I took advanced math and science courses throughout my school years that satisfied academic requirements and set me apart from my classmates. I knew it would help set the stage for what I wanted to achieve. In 1987, when I first heard Mae Jemison (the first female African American to go into space) had become one of the candidates NASA selected to enter training to become an astronaut, I was elated that a role model who shared my ethnicity, gender, and aspiration was on the path to accomplishing what I wanted. I followed Mae's progress as I left my home in Vicksburg, Mississippi to attend a magnet school in Columbus, Mississippi to enhance my education in eleventh grade. That forced me to grow up fast. From there, I attended the U.S. Naval Academy in Annapolis, Maryland (most astronauts at that time were trained in the U.S. Navy) through my sophomore year before moving on to Texas A&M University to finish college and earn my degree in mechanical engineering technology in 1995.

My time at the Academy provided much needed structure and discipline, and I successfully completed my first year there, which most consider to be the hardest. I am very proud of that accomplishment. However, toward the end of the following year, I began to experience severe medical issues. I was in and out of the hospital, and doctors could not determine the root cause. I did some soul searching and determined that I was sacrificing my health to get a better education. During this time, I leaned in to God and grew in my faith. It taught me that even when things don't turn out as I thought they would, His greater plan is still in motion. By the third hospital stay, I realized I wasn't going to go into space like Mae did aboard the Space Shuttle Endeavor in 1992, but I figured I'd do the next best thing as an engineer by helping send others into space and give myself more visibility within the field in the process. After leaving the Academy, I still had a few more medical episodes, but they eventually ended without ever being diagnosed. In the meantime, resiliency and determination became building blocks for my life—and they served as a catalyst for my desire to make "each one reach one" a reality.

Today, I am living my true calling to positively add value to the organizations I have worked for, and the people I have touched, by inspiring others to maximize their potential. God blesses me so that I can be a blessing to others. I continue to exemplify "each one reach one" as I listen to God and respond to the leading of the Holy Spirit. If I do both, then I know that I am in His will. At the advent of 2024, I have accomplished above and beyond what I thought I could do. Over the previous years I won both local and national awards in the diversity, equity, and inclusion arena. I did not do that alone. It takes a village, and every time someone tries to give me the credit, I communicate that I am standing on the shoulders of others who paved the way for me and lived out the principle of "each one reach one" in my life.

I have a variety of faith heroes, and each one inspires me in a different, but significant, way. My late distant cousin, Bettye Smith Brown, was like an aunt to me, and she emphasized getting an education, adding that my only limits were those I placed on myself. She called me her "phenomenal woman," in reference to the title and message of Maya Angelou's incredible poem. Though it speaks to the outer beauty one possesses, that poem taught me to be confident in who I am inside as well as outside. It also taught me that my uniqueness is to be valued, that it is okay to be different, and that I am enough. I can have my own energy and style, be confident in who I am, and be proud of myself, knowing that there is a lesson to be learned in everything.

John Murray Jr. is my father, and I must say I truly am a daddy's girl. When I was younger, he encouraged me to go to church and to develop a personal faith with God. After he and my mother divorced, and as I have matured, I now see in him a living example of the life he encouraged me to live. He completed an associate's degree in theology because he wanted to be able to understand the Bible better, and during the COVID-19 pandemic, he and I had Bible studies together over the phone. I know that my relationship with my earthly father is one reason my relationship with my Heavenly Father continues to grow today.

Mary Bush (I call her "Ma Bush") has been in my life for over 18 years, and I consider her to be my "bonus mom." She and I have been together on the mountain-top and shared our moments in the valley, yet we are still connected and there for one another. At the time of this writing, she was going through some medical challenges. We believe and know that God is a healer and that we have to walk in His promises for us.

I met Dr. Allison Alston at a conference, and I was immediately intrigued and wanted to get to know her. After a few calls, I knew I wanted to keep a relationship with her. We have supported each other in our day-to-day lives and in our faith journeys. Likewise, I met Dr. Amanda H. Goodson, co-author of this book, at a conference many years ago, and from then on it seemed that our paths kept crossing, like the Lord was orchestrating it all. Our bond has grown, and she has been instrumental in sharing various ways I could grow in my relationship with

God. Dr. Yvette Rice, the other co-author of this book, has also taken the time to encourage me, pour into me, and provide guidance on spiritual matters. I appreciate her so for the beautiful design she has imprinted on the tapestry of my faith. I'm proud to have joined with Drs. Goodson and Rice to start WeTECH Rocks, a consortium based on accelerating women in Science, Technology, Engineering and Mathematics (STEM) education.

Finally, I have been inspired by the faith heroes in the McKinney Fit Body Boot Camp (the gym group I mentioned at the beginning of this chapter). When we started, there was a common kinship between us, but no prayer. After we introduced prayer into our time together, the action took hold, adding a layer of unity between us that will undoubtedly last a lifetime.

Have you ever heard the joke, "If you want to hear God laugh, tell Him your plan?" As I have lived out my faith in the marketplace, I have learned God's plan is not my plan—or, better said, my plan is not His plan. Sarah learned this when she tried to take matters into her own hands, discovering that God didn't need her help to fulfill His promises.

He doesn't need our help, either. God has a plan for each and every one of us. When I think about the challenges I have experienced—my parents getting divorced, my days at the Naval Academy, my Six Sigma Black Belt certification journey, and a plethora of others—each time I made it through the valley, I gained a better understanding of why I had to go through that situation in the first place. There is always a reason why we face challenges, but that reason may not always be for us. Often, it is for someone else so they can have someone, in us, who they can comfortably relate to about their own feelings, experiences, and faith. Yet that insight only comes as we go through, not around, the circumstance. That's part of His plan. With each challenge, I have grown closer to God. I read, study, pray, and seek Him more.

My measure of success is to help others be their best selves. That requires me to live a life that is representative of how God wants to use me to draw others to Him and His kingdom. I once heard Christian comedian, Michael Jr., say that your "why" informs what you do and makes it more impactful. He says being a comedian is his "what," but his "why" is to inspire people to walk in purpose. Whatever else he does to support that, from writing books to being in motion pictures, is motivated by his "why."

I believe the best strategy for exercising faith in the marketplace is to know who you are and *whose* you are. Pay it forward by helping others. Remember that you did not magically arrive at your success all alone. Recall the mentors, coaches—the "village"—who helped you get to where you are today, and consider that there is more than enough to go around. Don't pull others down in order to elevate yourself. God will ultimately plant you where He wants you to be. Just as Sarah learned, trust in His plan, not yours.

Odetta Scott is an author, advisor, mentor, and lecturer who has fueled the development of individuals at all levels as well as driven transformational culture in professional and business settings.

Contact Odetta at:
https://www.linkedin.com/in/odetta-scott-58298513/

2

The Impossible is Possible!

Dr. Amanda H. Goodson

Leah

"May the Lord make the woman who is coming into your home like Rachel and Leah, who together built up the family of Israel."

(Ruth 4:11, NIV)

The strength, courage, and tenacity to believe the impossible.

That's what it means to have faith in the marketplace—to focus and get to that place where you are able to successfully exemplify your faith and operate in it with the attitude that great things can, and will, happen as you do.

This is not easy, but regardless of the season or what's changing in your life, it is empowered when you know who you are and *Whose* you are. My job is not my Lord. My boss is not my Lord. God is my Lord, and I do everything I can each day to remember that and live in its reality.

I've certainly lived in its blessing. God has enabled me to be a leader in a variety of venues as an engineer, leadership coach, teacher, speaker, and pastor. When I was growing up in the shadow of the U.S. Space and Rocket Center in Huntsville, Alabama, I never imagined the Lord would give me a career at the National Aeronautics and Space Administration (NASA) that included becoming the first African American woman to ever hold the position of Director of Safety and Mission Assurance at the Marshall Space Flight Center. I also never imagined that God would call me to become a pastor at a church far away from home in a place I never thought I'd live, Tucson, Arizona.

But see, He has taught me to believe the impossible is possible—and it's important to me to pass that forward because I've observed so many people who don't see themselves as capable of becoming great, much less extraordinary. As I wrote in my book, *Astronomical Leadership*, "We settle for being average. We think we are fine just the way we are. But I believe we are created to succeed. To excel. To *be* extraordinary."

There is a woman in the Bible who inspires me to have faith in whatever marketplace I am operating in. She certainly did so in her time and culture. Her name is Leah, and her story is found in Genesis 29-33. Those five chapters share the account of a woman that almost everybody had counted out, someone who certainly couldn't achieve the extraordinary. Although Leah was the oldest of two sisters, it was her younger, more attractive sibling, Rachel, who was chosen to become Jacob's wife, even though the custom at that time was for the older daughter to be wed first. Yet God, and Leah's father, Laban, orchestrated events so that Leah would not only be married first but would also become the mother to six sons for whom 12 of the tribes of the nation of Israel were named! Her father showed Leah favor. He didn't want her to go without a husband or lack the experiences a woman in her culture was supposed to have—and God favored Leah by blessing her with children which led to a mighty legacy as part of the genealogy of Jesus Christ.

Leah became one of the most influential women in the Bible, although it appeared that she wouldn't be much of an influence at all. Through it all, Leah was shown to have a personality that was supportive and stable, respectful and cautious, and that consistently took up for her family. She may have been viewed as plain and ordinary, but Leah was tenderhearted and amazingly strong in the face of dif-ficulty and discouragement. Because of these attributes, Leah received favor, and that favor was reproduced in her life to impact many other lives to come.

Like Leah, I have received favor from God that I have been privileged to reproduce in other's lives through my work, in my family, in the community, and through my church. I have also been honored to be a mentor to women in America and internationally who have reached out to me about how to live out their faith in the market-place. They want to grow, and they see an opportunity to develop themselves and their abilities and progress from crawling to walking to soaring to their destiny—achieving and believing that the impossible is possible!

This is never easy, and it will come with its set of obstacles to overcome. I will always remember my early days working for NASA at the Marshall Space Flight Center. A coworker named JMT had been hired for the same engineering intern position as me, but he had done some earlier summer work at NASA. I quickly identified him as someone I needed to know because he knew more about what was going on there than I did. As we got to know one another, JMT became a friend. Direct and truthful to a fault, he told me one afternoon, "The only reason you're here is because you're black. You know that, don't you? It's part of affirmative action."

"That's not true," I countered.

"Yes, it is. Go ask somebody. They'll tell you."

I knew he wasn't being mean, and certainly not racist. He was just telling it like it was, at least from his standpoint. But for me, it was the same thing all over again. From some teachers in elementary school to administrators in middle school and a counselor in high school, here was someone else suggesting that my race or gender, not my qualifications, was what got me where I was. I replied, "Well, we'll just see about that, JMT."

I considered going to my boss to see if the whole affirmative action thing was true, but I never did because it didn't really matter. I was at NASA—so instead of allowing JMT's words to discourage me, I used them for motivation. I wasn't going to let JMT, anyone, or anything else define me. Looking at where I was at that point of my life, I didn't realize that what I was doing at that moment was operating in faith. I just told myself, *They're not going to get the best of me. I'm going to do this!*

God had positioned me and favored me—and that was that. I was going to believe for the impossible.

Fast forward to a year or so later when I met with Wiley, the director of quality assurance at Marshall. He called me into his big office one afternoon to give him the latest update on an experiment I was working on. As I sat down across from him at the massive conference table, we had a pivotal conversation. It began with Wiley asking me an unexpected question.

"What do you want to do?" he asked.

"What do you mean?" I replied.

"I mean, what do you really want—here at NASA?"

I thought about it and heard a voice within exhort me. *Be bold.* I leaned forward in my chair. "I want your job."

"You want my job?"

"Yes, sir!"

He looked straight ahead, assessing me, but his gaze wasn't skeptical. It was credulous. Respectful.

"I want to take you seriously," he said. "I've been looking for someone to help, to create a legacy." He paused. "Okay. If you want my job, you're gonna have to work hard, do the jobs you never want to do, and do the jobs others are not willing to do."

Suddenly, I was the one challenged to take him seriously. "I can do all those things," I said.

He got up from his chair, and I rose from mine. "All right, then. I've got some work to do to make this happen."

As I left Wiley's office, my mind was buzzing. *I need to do what others can't. Do what others won't. Find a space where nobody is and cannot touch where I am.*

As I headed back toward my cubicle, I took a quick detour and found Inellia. She worked in human resources and had set herself apart as someone I could go to for advice. Inellia had a ready smile and possessed a humble boldness. She looked out for me and always had a word on how I could do something differently or better. I told her everything that had just happened with Wiley, including my declaration to take his job someday.

"If you're gonna do that, you really need to listen to what he says." Then she grinned. She didn't explicitly state it, but because of her position in human resources, she surely knew I'd be the first black woman to ever hold that directorship position if I got it.

Then she said, "The impossible might be possible."

The rest, as they say, is history. Wiley was true to his word. He sponsored me, and I did take his job. I progressed from there and ended up working on well over 30 Space Shuttle missions, experiencing many joys and some sorrows along the way, as a leader at NASA. Yet in every circumstance and difficulty, it was my growing faith that informed how I responded to those challenges in my marketplace to, as Inellia said, make the impossible possible.

That's what Leah did in her situation. She was her husband's second choice. Jacob's love for her sister, Rachel, was greater than his love for her (Genesis 29:30), and Leah surely felt that rejection. Yet in spite of what was going on around her, Leah kept moving forward in faith. She trusted God, and she did not allow her circumstances to take away from what she was bringing to her family.

It's interesting how, in Genesis 29:32-35, she vulnerably expressed her faith in the Lord in her difficulty. When Leah gave birth to her first son, Reuben, she said, "It is because the Lord has seen my misery. Surely my husband will love me now." Then, when her second child, Simeon, was born, Leah declared, "Because the Lord heard that I am not loved, he gave me this one too." Next came Levi, and Leah said, "Now at last my husband will become attached to me, because I have borne him three sons." Finally, at the birth of her fourth child, Judah, Leah announced, "This time I will praise the Lord."

Do you see the progression in her expressions of faith? Leah didn't deny the harsh reality of her position. She didn't think less of herself and cower down. Instead, Leah responded to her challenges with realistic, determined trust in God. At the same time, there were so many instances when Leah felt unworthy. She had what we today call "imposter syndrome," where part of her was bold while another part of her didn't think she deserved to be who she was. God had given Leah everything she needed to be successful in life, but she had not yet emerged from the external circumstances, and Jacob's persistent rejection of her, that pulled her back. She was seen as the lesser of the two sisters in terms of beauty and graces. She was treated as a second-class citizen in comparison to Rachel. Therefore, there was always competition between Leah and her sister.

I think of that progression in Leah's faith whenever I face hard business decisions in the marketplace. I recognize who I am and what the diversity of my skills and expertise brings to the situation, and I accelerate my way through it. Leah was able to accelerate herself throughout her joys and ordeals as Jacob's wife and as a mother. She allowed her experiences to propel her forward. I recall when I was offered a new role in 2021 that allowed me to continue working at my employer's Tucson offices, but also required nearly double the responsibilities of my previous position. Through that transition, God taught me that, if He has blessed us with a new or different assignment, we must move forward, march toward the mark, and operate in faith, so we don't get ahead of, or lag behind, what God is doing. I needed to be on pointe and in harmony with the symphonic movement of His Holy Spirit.

Vital to this is asking God what is on His *mind*, not what is in His *hand*. Even though the Lord is going to give us what's in His hand, we want to know His will for that particular season so that we can thrive in it. I can easily imagine Leah asking the Lord that exact question throughout her experiences. One time in particular came when she had to make a difficult transaction with Rachel. Genesis 30 describes how Rachel, who was unable to bear children and had become jealous of Leah, gave her servant to Jacob (a common practice in that culture). That servant bore Jacob two children on behalf of Rachel, and Rachel felt vindicated against Leah.

In response, Leah, who already had four biological children with Jacob, gave her servant to her husband for the same purpose. Leah's servant bore two children with Jacob, seemingly settling the score with her sister—but the contentiousness between Rachel and Leah continued anyway. No matter what she did, she knew Jacob wanted to be with her sister over her.

Leah's oldest son, Reuben, then came in from the fields with a batch of mandrake plants, which were believed to help women become more fertile. Rachel came to Leah and asked for the mandrakes, and Leah's core frustration boiled to the surface.

"Wasn't it enough that you took away my husband? Will you take my son's mandrakes too?" she asked Rachel.

"Very well," Rachel said, "he can sleep with you tonight in return for your son's mandrakes."

Leah agreed to the exchange so that she could conceive once again with Jacob. She then had three more biological children, two sons and a daughter. Meanwhile, Rachel was finally able to conceive with Jacob, and she had a son.

Leah followed God's leading in her life to pursue what she wanted. She also emerged from her imposter syndrome to become the woman God purposed her to be as He blessed her as the mother of the tribes of Israel, His chosen people. Sadly, the Bible never reports whether Jacob ever grew to love Leah—but Leah was certainly loved by God and was positioned by Him to help achieve His will. Later, when Jacob had a fateful meeting with his brother Esau, as told in Genesis 33, he placed Leah and her children in line *before* Rachel and her son, Joseph. While this positioning likely placed Leah in slightly more danger as Esau and his men approached them, I believe this also worked to end Leah's imposter syndrome. Leah also ended up outliving Rachel, and she was honored equally with Rachel as the two women who "built up the family of Israel." (Ruth 4:11)

It is clear from Leah's story that there were many moments when life must've felt unfair. It happens to all of us. During those times in my life, I try to see things from the other person's lily pad. I think to myself, *They must be going through some really tough times. How may I extend grace to them?* I've had a lot of conversations like this with myself. They help me realize that what I see is not equal to what I know. Therefore, I need to go with what I know, not what I see. We must always take ourselves beyond what we see—the unfairness, the injustice, whatever it may be—to focus on what we know.

As I consider how my faith has grown my capabilities, skills, and results in the marketplace, I've determined that it is manifested in knowing what to do at any period of time. For example, I might have a project that requires me to read hundreds of pages of documents, so I need to know specifically what I need to learn from that research. I am able to do that only by operating in the power and strength of Jesus Christ. That's where the anointing comes for me to get the results God expects, which, of course, will affect my effectiveness at work and my ability to give my bosses what they need. I am also careful to nurture a relationship with those in leadership over me by giving them encouragement and comfort while exhorting them, even when things are not going well. When a project is succeeding, I am sure to highlight what I really like about it and other people in the organization, as well as mentioning what they did well as supervisors. I bring all of that to the forefront so that we can all celebrate together.

Whenever I face professional disappointments, I look to God as the author and the finisher of my faith (Hebrews 12:2). He is my strong tower (Proverbs 18:10 who will protect me and never put more on me than I can bear (1 Corinthians 10:13). I don't look to the left or the right, only straight ahead at Him (Proverbs 4:25-27), trusting that, whatever the situation, "this, too, shall pass." I just keep moving.

Leah did this. She was a powerhouse to stay where she was in the midst of her many disappointments. Steadfast and determined, Leah leaned on her ability to be a mother, knowing she was a blessing to her children despite being rejected by Jacob. Leah didn't rebel. She realigned herself. It was like she knew God had spoken to her and winked her way by giving her all those children. She knew God was watching her and that He was with her, and she held on to that. There was only one source of truth for her, and it was God.

In my career at NASA, I leaned on God through two heartbreaking disappointments involving the Space Shuttle program. Even though much of the work I did during my first two-and-a-half years at the Marshall Space Flight Center supported the shuttle program, I had watched only a few launches. The next one, in January 1986, had garnered more national attention because it was going to be the first one to take a civilian, a school-teacher, into space, but I couldn't see it anyway. I was in a training class, along with nearly 200 other workers from throughout the Huntsville business community, and away from the televisions in the lobby.

I had been in some pre-flight or post-flight meetings at Marshall regarding shuttle missions, but only as a spectator, not as an active participant. I'd never worked a launch and didn't know details about launches. Yet the destruction of the Space Shuttle Challenger during its launch that morning rocked me. The shuttle and its crew were gone, and no one knew why. Shortly after the disaster, my colleagues and I at Marshall combed through flight data from the Challenger payload and other electronic information. It was all-hands-on-deck and stayed that way for nearly two years. We examined. We analyzed. We assessed. We worked hard.

After a while, we started projects on shuttle bay items for the next flight, whenever that was going to be. My job was all-consuming—yet I thrived through that disappointment. I worked on my master's program and began taking additional classes on leadership while continuing to set myself apart from my colleagues. I was motivated by standards, goals, strategies, and tactical execution at a greater level than those around me. Later, I was given an active role in determining the type of O-ring, the circular gaskets that kept gases from escaping from the shuttle's solid rocket boosters, that should be used on future shuttle missions.

The second disappointment, described in heartbreaking detail in the opening chapter of *Astronomical Leadership*, came in February 2003 with the destruction during reentry of STS-107, the Space Shuttle Columbia, as it sped home to land at the Kennedy Space Center in Florida. I had been Director of Safety and Mission Assurance for seven years, and my team and I oversaw propulsion systems for the shuttle program with direct responsibility for shuttle launches. While we weren't involved with reentry or landings, the utter shock of the disaster shook me to my very core. We had learned some harsh lessons from the Challenger disaster, and I was among those who painstakingly labored to solve the issues that caused that explosion. We had seen so many successful missions since then.

But this? I thought that horrible morning in 2003. *It just couldn't be happening again.*

On the way to my office at the flight center in Huntsville, I knew I couldn't slide further into dejection. Determinedly, I snapped into automatic mode and systematically thought through every necessary step to ensure I was going to be ready when I walked into that room to deal with what had just happened.

Still, at a stoplight close to Marshall, I peered up at the sky through my windshield and allowed myself to think of the seven-member crew of Columbia. There were two women, one of whom was India's first shuttle astronaut; an Israeli Air Force colonel, and son of a Holocaust survivor, who was that nation's first astronaut; and an African American payload commander. Columbia's commander was Rick

Husband—who I had lunch with a few years before the launch. We talked to each other about the mission and our respective families, but more than anything, I wanted him to know how thankful and appreciative I was for what he did as a NASA astronaut—and rest assured knowing his safety, and that of his crew, was my priority.

"The first eight-and-a-half minutes after launch, I got you," I said. It wasn't a cocky statement, but one born from confidence in myself and the ability of my team.

He nodded his head. "Amanda," he said simply, "thank you for doing your best."

Rick Husband was a gentleman and one of the kindest people I ever met. I had no doubt he appreciated and respected me and the duties and difficulties of my position at NASA, and I knew his reply was genuine. But I also sensed that he wanted me to understand that I didn't have control over everything that could happen during the launch or at any other point of a shuttle mission. He, like all the other astronauts I'd been privileged to meet, understood that space exploration was a dangerous business. There was no such thing as a guarantee.

That reality did nothing to alleviate the sorrow I felt that very moment in my car.

The rest of the story, as told in *Astronomical Leadership*, tells how we went to work, investigated the accident, and identified what caused it. After the Columbia disaster, the next space shuttle flight wasn't until July 2005. Yet I wasn't there for that. Just weeks before the release of the first volume of the accident investigation board's report in August 2003, I had already left NASA, never to return.

———————

The lessons I learned at NASA, however, have never left me. Art Stephenson, the ninth director of the Marshall Space Flight Center, played a pivotal role in my career. He helped me to understand the role of a coach as a leader, and I will always be thankful for his humility and servant leadership. In his book *Out of the Blue*, Stephenson shared his life story from boyhood to retirement. He wrote that there were times God was moving on his behalf and he had no clue that what he was going through was going to help him with the next dimension of his life. In those moments, he said people should be led by their values, even when those values sometimes compete with one another. For example, Family First is a value. Hard Work is another value, and Results Driven is a third. However, he taught me if something critical is going on with our family, hard work and results may have to take a second seat.

There were surely times Leah had no clue that what she was going through was going to help her with the next things God had in store in her life, yet she trusted Him—and He, in turn, valued her. God values us as well. We won't always see what He is doing in our lives in our current circumstances, but we need to trust He is there. We may not see it, but our option is to *believe* it. Then, when He is lifted up and made known through what He had done in our lives, we can raise our hands to heaven and say, "God, you see what they said about you? Allow this to glorify you!" When this happens to me, I love to have a conversation with God, praise Him, and let Him know, "Hey, this is you. Hallelujah, God!"

God has often wowed me in my career as a woman of faith in the marketplace. He has given me many great opportunities to travel and live in different places. I never expected that when I was growing up. I never thought I'd have so many chances to represent Him and help other people. Often, they didn't expect that help, but once I was in that "seat" where I could benefit them, they recognized why God had me there for them. The Lord is saying, "Take your seat," meaning to sit down and do what He calls us to do, and incredible things will follow.

As I look back at some of my faith heroes such as Myles Munroe, Max Lucado, John C. Maxwell, and Cindy Trimm, I believe the best advice I've ever learned is to not compare myself with someone else, but to create my own opportunities. As I look at only what I can do, it takes everyone else off the table, and I'm no longer competing. Instead, I'm *completing* what God has called me to do. The best opportunities I've had to excel and expand God's Kingdom have come by making a difference right where I am. God has given me His favor to go up and up and up! Why? I trust God, and He trusts me.

My measure of success is to represent God's Kingdom government here on earth in a way that points directly to Christ. When people see me, they see Jesus. I may not say His name, but they observe the characteristics of Christ. Whenever I make a mistake, I own up to it and get back on the road. So, my faith strategy in the marketplace is to represent Christ, being bold as a lion and gentle as a dove, striving to make myself relatable and relevant in every aspect of what I bring to the table: to encourage, exhort, and equip people and let them know they are important in every way.

Take your place and be the person God has called you to be—whether that be bold and influential, steady and supportive, deep in technical skills, or concise and analytical. Bring that to the table, represent God, and always point to Christ.

The impossible *is* possible to you!

Dr. Amanda H. Goodson is a groundbreaking aerospace engineer who soared to become the first woman to hold the position of Director of Safety and Mission Assurance out of the Marshall Space Flight center at NASA. Transformed from a young African American girl who was told by her teacher that she would not amount to much, Dr. Goodson uses her unstoppable "can do" spirit to inspire others to achieve their goals regardless of the obstacles.

Noted nationally for her achievements, Dr. Goodson has served on the Board of Director's Chair for Advancing Minorities Interest in Engineering (AMIE) in addition to serving in leadership positions for a Fortune 500 aerospace company. Dr. Goodson is also the Senior Pastor at New Trinity Temple CME church in Tucson, Arizona.

Contact Amanda at www.amandagoodson.com

3

Live in Victory: The Five Cs of Faith

Elisa Marchetti (Lisa)

Deborah

"Wake up, wake up, Deborah! Wake up, wake up, break out in song!"

(Judges 5:12, NIV)

What does "Live in Victory" mean to you? As a results-driven human resources leader, executive coach, and author, I've spent most of my career leading change management initiatives, partnering with leaders, and turning dysfunctional teams into high performing ones. Most of these initiatives are quantified to impact shareholder value and help the organization reach a measurement of victory. However, shareholder value is only one aspect of something greater and more connected. From there, it propels forward into expanding customer value and enhancing employee value, leading to increased community value that ultimately multiplies "Kingdom value" through faith in the marketplace. Even when difficult professional or personal decisions are presented and it might not feel like your most victorious moment, you are uniquely valued by God and we can "Live in Victory" every day because of the hope of Jesus.

In the past, I've been fortunate to have worked for two Fortune 500 companies and a family-owned business. Currently, my role at a large aerospace and defense company centers on organizational effectiveness, shaping employee listening strategies. Through my team, we analyze our employees' insights, compiling both quantitative and qualitative data to ensure that the voices of our employees are heard and represented to enhance the employee experience and spur action through business decisions.

Then and now, in all that I do, I have an anchor that determines who I am—and I feel that it also defines faith in the marketplace. It's in the New Testament, and it declares, "Whatever you do, work at it with all your heart, as working for the Lord, not for human masters." (Colossians 3:23, NIV) Those who have grown up in a family-owned business like I did know that, regardless of personal birth order, skills, or traits in the family, there is a role (even if it feels small) for everyone to contribute to the business. This is good news for all of us because, as part of God's family, all of us have a role in our Father's business—to make Kingdom impact.

I may work for other leaders, a hierarchy in the organization, where it seems like someone else is in charge of strategy or execution, but this anchoring verse reminds me that God is my authority and my boss. Everything we do is the Lord's, everything I do is working for Him, and we get to have a part in the family business.

There's a woman in the Old Testament who I believe was an anchor in her "marketplace" and for her people. She steadfastly anchored herself in God as her sole authority and certainly made a Kingdom impact. Deborah was a judge and a leader, but the Bible first mentions her being a prophetess and a wife. I also believe she was a nurturing mother for her people and a warrior for justice and courage who operated as an advocate with great discernment and compassion.

I admire Deborah, and as I considered the characteristics she demonstrated in her life, I've picked five of them—I call them the "Five Cs of Faith"—that are relevant for us today as we seek to exemplify our faith in the marketplaces where we serve.

- Conflict management.
- Compassion.
- Courage.
- Collaboration.
- Confidence.

Deborah's story in Judges chapters 4-5 brings out each incredible faith trait.

1. CONFLICT MANAGEMENT

Deborah held her court under "the Palm of Deborah" in the hill country of Ephraim, and the people of Israel constantly went to her to have their disputes decided (Judges

4:5). She served as mediator as they brought their conflicts before her, and Deborah had to practice a core discipline of conflict management: discerning when to escalate and when to de-escalate. We need to know how to be calm and keep things stable, but we also need to understand when It is appropriate to charge the hill and move forward. Deborah did that very well, always balancing escalation and de-escalation expertly.

Any marketplace leader in corporate America will face conflict. In my role in human resources, I am a mediator who helps to bring people together, in areas where they only see differences, in order to broker a solution between them. I work with some very strong leaders. Any time there is a conflict, even if it feels minor, there is something to work through on a personal level. There may be a history, sometimes a really deep-rooted history, of disrespect or of feeling like someone did not hold up their end of the bargain. In these situations, I ask both parties three main questions—ones I encourage anybody to use in the marketplace or in their personal life.

Look the other person in the eye and then reflect on the following:

1. What do you need from the other person? What is the unmet expectation? It could be that they need to stop being passive-aggressive or that they need to try to communicate better and share their strategies so that it doesn't feel like there is a personal agenda in play. Articulate the unmet expectation.

2. What does the other person need from you? Maybe they need more information. Perhaps they need space. Are you micromanaging a little too much and need to back off? Do they need you to have

positive intent instead of a negative approach? Look beyond yourself to understand what they want.

3. Then comes the most important question. Is it reconcilable? If the answer is "no," spend your energy figuring out how someone can move to a different department, role, or job. Typically, though, the conflict can be resolved. In nearly 20 years, I have had only two instances where executive leaders concluded that they could not reconcile.

Deborah serves as my example of how to do this effectively and with Godly wisdom. She heard both parties and asked thought-provoking questions to start successfully moving through conflict. She wasn't ruffled. She was calm. Because of the respect Deborah had built as a leader, she knew how to use empathy to understand people and see the situation from both sides.

2. COMPASSION

Deborah demonstrated compassion as an advocate for others and for herself. She spoke quite a bit about how she loved the Lord, her people, and preserving the Israelite's legacy in the famous Song of Deborah in Judges 5. I particularly love her words in verse 14 of that chapter. "My heart is with Israel's princes, with the willing volunteers among the people."

In certain roles throughout my career, I've been in unique positions where I was given a broader perspective that others couldn't see. In these situations, there was a blockage or a barrier in the way. Through advocacy and compassion, I was able to bring those obstacles to light to preserve and protect those who couldn't adequately speak or lobby for themselves.

Of course, in order to show compassion, we have to experience it ourselves. Once we do, we can understand and show it to others. There is a place for compassion in all of our relationships at work, with our friends, and within the family. When I was eight years of age, I was diagnosed as a Type 1 diabetic. Today, medical technology is advanced. I can use an insulin pump with continuous glucose monitoring, so if I eat more sugar than I should, I can quickly adjust and give myself more insulin. Back when I was diagnosed, though, I had to take several shots of insulin a day, pricking my finger and literally putting a drop of my blood on a stick to test my sugar level. As a family, we had to dive in and figure out how to manage it.

We didn't understand carbohydrates and sugars as well as we do now, so there were things I simply could not eat. Before I knew I had diabetes, my sister, Mandy, and I used to ride our bikes to the local deli and get Laffy Taffy to eat while we were riding back home. When that was not possible anymore, we would ride to the deli, and I'd get my second favorite snack, a Slim Jim. It was an acceptable substitute for the candy, but I still struggled with temptation. As a kid, it was hard not to want to indulge. I felt like I deserved to and wondered why I couldn't. Then Girl Scout Cookie season rolled around, and I *loved* Thin Mints. Just because I was diabetic didn't mean everyone else had to stay away from sugar, so we had them in the house.

One day after school, Mandy and I were playing outside in the snow, and I just couldn't take it anymore. I told her I needed to go inside to use the restroom, but when I took longer than expected to return, Mandy came inside—only to find me actually in the kitchen, hiding behind the pantry closet door, munching away on Thin Mints. Typically, the cookies were way at the top where I couldn't reach them, but someone else must've eaten some and left them on one of the lower shelves.

"What are you doing?" Mandy exclaimed. Her voice was almost a whisper.

I peeped in surprise, my heart pounding. I realized chocolatey crumbs were on my lips.

"Did you eat the cookies?" she asked quietly.

"Yes," I admitted, my eyes tearing up. "I couldn't help myself."

I started crying. I was embarrassed and ashamed.

Mandy knew I couldn't eat the cookies. She could have told our parents, and I would have been in really big trouble. But Mandy showed incredible compassion. We put the mints away, walked out of the kitchen, and she gave me a hug as we went back outside to play.

"Don't worry," she assured me. "I won't tell mom and dad."

I'm sure they knew something was up later that night because my blood sugar must have been very high. They likely wondered what happened. Yet in that moment, as I sat in the pantry giving in to temptation, my sister chose to show compassion instead of judging me and tattling.

In the marketplace, there will be times that we are uniquely positioned, just as my sister was with me, to stand in a place of compassion. At a prior employer, a medical device company, I was the human resources partner for the sales department. Our salespeople had a specific compensation plan, based on how much they sold, that was different from the rest of the company because they were driving revenue. We got through the fiscal year and were running our final numbers when one of our finance reps came to me with shocking news.

There had been a mistake on the commission plans. We had overpaid some of our salespeople and underpaid others. Incorporating several factors including tangible and intangible costs, it was a large financial impact.

It was a serious moment. On one end of the table was the chief financial officer saying, "We overpaid people. They have to pay it back." On the other side was the vice president of sales countering, "I am going to have a complete retention risk if you tell some of our hard-working salespeople that they have to give it back." One was proposing, "Forgive the debt. It was our mistake." The other was admitting, "Yes, this was our mistake, but at the end of the day it is not equitable, and it causes a problem with the entire sales force. We have to pay people the way we committed to do."

My boss stepped in, and I saw her compassion. She formed a team, and we worked through the situation, so we could get the money back from the affected salespeople in a variety of different ways and make it right for the people who were underpaid. The company also took a level of accountability. It was hard to walk alongside the sales team as they were given difficult news that they did not cause. We had to stand in the gap and work through a compassionate solution that still held the company line and ensure that there were additional checks and balances, so it wouldn't happen again.

3. COURAGE

Deborah was the leader of her people while Barak was appointed head of the Israelite army. When she called

Barak to her and commanded him to take his fighters to find those who were oppressing the Israelites and battle them, his response was telling. "If you go with me, I will go; but if you don't go with me, I won't go." (Judges 4:8, NIV) I believed Barak so respected Deborah's authority and courage that he didn't want to go to war unless she was by his side. He knew he couldn't do it without her, and in turn, she respected his role and his strengths and knew she could not accomplish victory without him. Deborah was a warrior, so she enthusiastically agreed to go with him and the army (Judges 4:9). It ended up being *the* moment the Israelites stood strong and honored the Lord, even after they had disappointed God time and again in the past through their disobedience.

Deborah didn't just sit back and tell the people what to do. She had the courage to speak up and act! When I think about today's marketplace, there are times when we need to stand up for those who are being oppressed or ill-treated, for those who God has placed on our heart, and when there is an injustice, we need to lead in word and action. She had full confidence in who she was, and she stood up for the things she believed in, including other people.

Having courage for others in the marketplace often means standing up and being there for them when nobody else can. They may not be in a position where they can escalate the situation or speak for themselves to those who are the decision makers. In human resources, I get the opportunity to have a bird's eye view of the business and interact with all levels of employees. Sometimes, I am able to pitch the ideas and proposals of others to influence executives who want to listen and learn more.

In the medical device company that I mentioned earlier, there were clinical specialists, who typically had a nursing or physical therapist background, whose roles were often viewed as secondary and perhaps even misperceived as being less important than the salespeople who were driving the revenue. They weren't as visible and didn't seem as glamorous as those in sales, but the clinical workers were the heartbeat of what the company achieved and were responsible for patient outcomes. There were many career paths, rewards, and promotional opportunities for the sales representatives, who were well-deserving, and we certainly did not want to take anything away from them. Through data, we discovered that some of the most successful sales regions were those that had also established a strong relationship and partnership between the sales representatives and their clinical specialists. There were many intangible things a clinical specialist did that couldn't be directly tied to revenue, so it was difficult to make a strong, quantitative correlation to increased compensation. However, the success of the sales and clinical specialist partnership was an indisputable qualitative key performance indicator. Partnerships are key. Deborah had a partnership with Barak. Each one of them was necessary and needed.

In partnership with my boss, we were able to be the voice of the specialists to leadership, having courage, on their behalf, to argue for their value to the company. They needed to feel that they were cared about and had a future in the organization because the skills they brought to the company were just as valuable as those of the salespeople. We also wanted to create career paths, rewards, and promotional opportunities for the clinical specialists. Through this business initiative, we created a path that allowed a clinical specialist to move upward to senior, principal, and leadership positions, providing career advancement and opportunities for greater financial rewards. I'm pleased to say, a decade after leaving that company, the clinical specialist career path still exists and has been advanced, not only impacting those who were chosen as the first cohort, but also those who are in those roles today. It has had a ripple effect and positively impacted their families and the company, and it has had a greater impact on the patients they serve, expanding employee, customer, and community value.

4. COLLABORATION

Not only was there collaboration in Judges 4 between Deborah and the leader of her army, but another collaborator rose up, a woman named Jael, who literally struck the key blow against the leader of the Israelite's enemies (Judges 4:17-22). Deborah sang Jael's praises in Judges 5:24-27, calling her "most blessed of women" as she described how Jael was used by God to help deliver the people. Throughout her story, Deborah never said she'd do anything on her own. She didn't have a personal agenda. She partnered with others and desired to strengthen them through her leadership.

Collaboration is influencing through strengthening others. We never really do anything alone. We always need to collaborate with and impact those around us at work, at home, and in our communities. We are all interdependent on each other in the marketplace. You can't do any work all by yourself. The best teams I've been part of, those I've seen who have strength in each other, succeeded through collaboration.

Organizations often have team building events or getaways designed to help their employees grow and develop into a high performing group. I was involved in one such team building exercise where four teams were each tasked with building a bicycle. It was set up like a competition with teams competing for bike parts. Since each team had to build a bike, it seemed the collaboration was only going to be within the individual teams. But as the activity progressed, its real purpose became obvious. One team ended up with two handlebars. Another had three tires. It became clear that each team had something another team lacked. The teams, therefore, had to work collectively to construct the four bikes.

It was an incredible experience because sometimes in life it's easy to think of others like, *They are the competition. They are not like me. They are different from me. This is my group, and this is it.* Yet if you lift your head, you realize that every one of us has strengths others need and weaknesses that others can make up for. We're better collectively than individually. Sure, there may be people you need to work with who you didn't choose to be on your team or others you may not like who have something you need. But we're stronger together.

As I work to create and execute an employee listening strategy with my current employer, I have many team members who are contributing to the effort because they possess unique strengths that are vital to our success. We need each other to accomplish what we desire to do.

5. CONFIDENCE

Deborah knew what she was called to do, but more than that, she knew who she was. She was a child of God, and that reality was her anchor. She had many roles: wife, mother, leader. She knew all those hats and how to wear them. Like Deborah, I am a wife, a mother, and a professional worker. I'm a leader and a volunteer. I know who I am, and I'm rooted in that, but above all, I'm a child of God—and confidence comes with that. You, too, are a chosen child of God, even as you wear multiple hats and fill many roles.

Before my husband, Alex, and I had children, we had three dogs, and I'll never forget our first dog. We got her from a litter of pups made available to us by Alex's friend. As we went to see the puppies, we were told that a few of them had already been chosen by others. When I walked into the yard, there were several dogs running around—and there she was, the runt of the litter. She was the smallest puppy, and she certainly wasn't the strongest, but she was sitting about two feet from me and just looked up at me with eyes that sparked an immediate connection. Pet lovers know exactly what that is like. There was no mistake about it. She was perfect just the way she was, and she was meant to be *our* dog. We named her Bailey.

I think that's often the way it is with us and God. We may feel like the runt of the litter, not the strongest or most qualified. We may even have imposter syndrome, thinking we've been thrown into a role and are the worst person for the job or being convinced we don't know what we're doing but acting like we do. Yet as we make ourselves available to God and choose to trust Him, *He picks us*, gathers us into His arms, and uses us for the task He has set aside just for us. If you struggle with thinking you aren't good enough, I want you to know God is saying to you, "There is something special about you. I picked you for this job. It is no mistake." God has uniquely created you for this moment in time to interact with others in a way that'll impact His Kingdom!

In addition, in a marketplace culture where we hear a lot about work-life balance, God will help you find the ideal balance to manage the task He's chosen you to do. There have been moments in my career when I didn't feel like I was performing my best at work or couldn't be as present as I should've been at home. Those were the times when God reminded me that I was hand chosen by Him, and He helped me make the small adjustments necessary to find my work-life balance and rediscover the confidence I needed to complete the job He had called me to do.

———————

Deborah influenced others and fulfilled that aspect of God's plan for her life, in a way that strengthened those around her. I believe everyone who came to her, from the people who came with conflicts, to Barak, Jael, and everyone in the Israelite army, was empowered by Deborah's leadership. She didn't influence others in order to fulfill her own feelings or desires. It was all based instead on what God put on her heart. I imagine there were moments when she encountered resistance, yet Deborah showed a compelling and humble confidence to lead and support the people, even to the point of going into battle with them.

Professionally or personally, there will be times when we are led into something uncomfortable or difficult, a pivotal point that may seem like a mountain that cannot be moved. This happened in my life when I heard the horrific words, "Your child has cancer." My son, Sal, was six at the time. Both Alex and I had professional careers that were going strong. Then, in one earthshattering instant, we thought our life as we knew it was over. I remember sitting in the hospital thinking we were going to lose everything. On top of the foremost concern about my son's health, I thought about the practical repercussions of his cancer battle. Giving up my job. Downsizing our house. Losing my time, energy, and freedom as I dealt with doctor's appointments and everything else that came with the situation. As everything was becoming cautious and scary, I was worried I'd lose my carefree spirit.

Then, in the middle of Sal's cancer journey, we got the awful news that Alex had cancer, too! Both my son and my husband were battling for their lives—and I did not know how either of their stories were going to end. Yet through the many twists and turns of their different journeys, which I share in my book, *Victory is Ahead: Dare to Hope*, God continued to show His strength and His love for us. During those times, I recalled Deborah and how she assured Barak she would go into battle with him—and I realized God was telling me the same thing. I thought of Deuteronomy 31:8, which says, "The Lord himself goes before you and will be with you; he will never leave you nor forsake you. Do not be afraid; do not be discouraged."

As of this writing in the summer of 2023, Sal and Alex were both in remission, and I praise God for that incredible gift! However, just because the cancer was no longer present didn't mean there weren't other unseen battles to face. Life did not go back to the way it was before. I am no longer the adventurous, carefree, risk-taking mom I used to be. I can still be fun, but I'm cautious. Every day, I ask myself, "What else?" "What if?" But I am more grounded and anchored in the Lord, and I still choose to trust in God and His sovereignty because He has shown His kindness to my family and me.

Maybe you find yourself facing the unexpected in this season of life. Perhaps a curve ball has been thrown your way. Devastation, grief, and despair might be creeping in. May I encourage you to cling to Deuteronomy 31:8? It's exhortation to not be afraid or discouraged is an anchor during the valleys of life, as well as when you feel like you are on the mountaintop with the sun shining on your face. Nothing is unexpected to God. He goes with you and is before you. You are equipped to face whatever may come—even cancer. We hold onto the victorious hope of salvation through Jesus Christ.

———————

Of course, glorifying the Lord when things are going well and I feel like I'm on top is best done with an attitude of humility. After all, none of us get to the top alone. A series of other people help us along the way. My parents have really shown and instilled in me what it means to walk by faith. Whether it has been in my personal or professional life, I have looked to their faith and seen how they have ministered to me and others. In addition, I am the youngest of four. I have two older brothers and Mandy, my older sister. My siblings have been good examples of how to keep walking the journey of life in the highs and in the lows. Then there was Deborah, who certainly wasn't given any easy cards to play, yet her faith was exemplary. She glorified God in praise and worship in Judges 5.

When things are going well for you, don't forget to enjoy it. Sometimes, we think we don't want to show it too much or be too grateful. If you are having a great day, it's okay to shout it out and be thankful for the good season! Humbly but confidently, show your gratitude and joy! I had the opportunity to do just that when I was an undergraduate pursuing my degree in business and marketing.

The spring of my junior year, I took an economics course, and my professor was tough. There was one particular test that I knew was going to be challenging, and I studied hard. Despite my efforts, I got a C, and I was crushed. I felt the work I put into my essay and responses deserved a better grade, so I set up a time to meet with my professor.

As I was on my way to her office, I mentally wrestled with a different issue: a desire to study abroad. I had applied for the opportunity, but by the time I did, I had missed the deadline. I was so sad about that, and my poor grade on the economics test only added to my sense of frustration.

The professor and I had a really good conversation about how and why I felt my grade was unfair. We met for over an hour, and she did two things. First, she decided to change my grade on my test to an A, saying she appreciated how I was able to professionally escalate the issues I brought up and articulate my points. Second, she told me about a study abroad program to China she was sponsoring—and she invited me to be one of the nine hand-selected students to take part.

She had no idea I wanted to study abroad! I said "yes" right then and there.

God is in the details! He knew my heart and my restlessness to see the world, but I couldn't do it on my own. I had to have that situation with my test, and the meeting with the the professor that followed, to make it happen! The test seemed to be a significant setback, and not only to that day. I thought it was going to ruin my college grades. I was probably being a bit dramatic feeling like that one grade was going to set me on a downward trajectory. However, setbacks sometimes become progress in disguise.

I returned to my dorm room and thanked the Lord with joy-filled humility. Not only did He know my tiniest dreams, but now I was grateful for the same professor I had been angry with an hour earlier. Again, progress can often seem like a setback at first.

————————

My favorite job in the whole wide world is being a mom—and I also see it as my greatest opportunity to expand God's Kingdom in this world. The number one thing I have the privilege and responsibility to do as a mother is to teach my son about Jesus. God is the sovereign giver of faith, so that is not up to me. But I can love and teach him about Christ, much as Deborah did as a mother and nurturer to the people of Israel. Scripture doesn't tell us if she was a biological mother, but that's not the point. All of us can invest our time, love, and faith into the next generation, whether or not we are actually parents to a child. We can teach colleagues about Jesus in the business world through mentorship, guidance, and taking an interest in others. It can be someone we like or dislike. Either way, they are worthy of being invested in, and our role is to advance them forward.

I look at it this way. Even if my corporate job changes tomorrow, that is not what makes me "me." As a child of God, He has given me other people with whom I can share the love of Jesus. You have them, too. Remembering the exhortation from Colossians 3:23 that serves as my anchor when defining faith in the marketplace, God is our authority. Whatever we do, we do for Him. After all, we're in our Father's business. Yet it's not just about what we do. It is who we *belong to.* We are His, created by Him for greatness and victory!

Finally, my measure of success as a woman in the marketplace is to keep the faith and finish the race set before me. It's grounded in Hebrews 12:1 where the Apostle Paul talks about running the course of our lives with perseverance, fixing our eyes on Jesus as "the author and finisher" of our faith.

That always makes me think back to high school. I participated in several sports, but track was my main event. I did the 300 and 400 meter hurdles. The longer race is one full lap around the track. I'm convinced humans were not biologically created to sprint that far. We can for 100 or 200 meters, but to run as fast as possible for 400 meters is pure grit. The first hundred you're thinking, "I got this," and by the second hundred you're still okay. Then, at 300 meters, you're going through the last turn before hitting the straight away with 100 meters to go. The tape at the finish line looks like it's a thousand miles away. You can't even feel your legs at that point, and your mind is screaming at you. *Stop! You've hit the wall. It's too hard. You can't make it. You're not good enough.*

That's why my coach was always right there on the infield as I came around the final turn, yelling one thing: "Lisa, pump your arms! Pump your arms!" He knew the faster I pumped my arms, the faster my legs would go, and his words kept me focused on that one thing.

In Hebrews 12:1, Paul is our coach—but instead of hollering, "Pump your arms!" Paul is saying, "Fix your eyes! Fix your eyes on Jesus!"

We are certain to succeed in business and in life as we work for the Lord with all of our heart, practice the "Five Cs of Faith," and keep our eyes fixed on Jesus.

Elisa Marchetti (Lisa) is a gifted speaker, a human resources leader, and an executive coach who passionately supports multiple non-profit childhood cancer organizations. She has worked for two Fortune 500 companies, holds a bachelor of science in marketing, and an MBA from Azusa Pacific University. She has authored two books. Her first book, *Victory is Ahead: Dare to Hope*, received Amazon Best Seller and Amazon #1 New Release honors. Currently, Lisa and her family reside in Dallas, Texas. She provides hope-filled leadership lessons and this constant reminder: "You are not alone in your trials. We hold onto victory through Jesus."

Contact Lisa at VictoryAhead318@gmail.com or www.victoryisahead.com

4

Every Single Thing

Je're Harmon

Ruth

"'I will do whatever you say,' Ruth answered."

(Ruth 3:5, NIV)

As Personnel Clearance Data Analytics Lead at a Fortune 200 technology company, my entire job is built on faith and trust. My daily duties to complete applications to obtain work clearances on contracts while maintaining metrics and dashboards using data analytics have allowed God to place me in a position where I help vet people to see if they are trustworthy to perform the duties our company requires. Therefore, it is critical that my team and I operate with integrity so that when we perform our assignments, we do them correctly and to the best of our abilities. After all, our company's partners trust us to do exactly that.

Therefore, my faith allows me to engage with the people I work with and the clients we serve. I have to trust and believe what God has spoken about me and what His Word says about me: that I am chosen by Him and fearfully and wonderfully made in His image. My job is not about getting paid. It is an assignment that God has given me to be part of that particular department and in that particular organization. Every day, God wants me to use my assignment there to impact His Kingdom and do the work He has called me to do.

I don't just go to work, and I don't just go for Je're. My work is a representation of my family, my church, my community, and ultimately, of Christ. Every single thing belongs to Him.

It's no wonder, then, that the woman of faith in the Bible who I most resonate with is Ruth. For me to be where I am, I have to be willing to receive a lot of guidance from different people. Actually, everywhere I have gone in my career is the result of the coaching, mentorship, and sponsorship of others. When I look at Ruth's story, as told in the Old Testament book that bears her name, it's clear that she was mentored and coached by her mother-in-law, Naomi.

The backstory is incredible and tragic. The book of Ruth starts with Naomi, her husband, Elimelech, and her two sons living in Bethlehem during a famine. A devoted wife, Naomi followed her husband to the foreign country of Moab to escape the famine and save their family. Shortly after arriving in Moab, Naomi's husband died. Although her sons took care of her and eventually married two Moabite women, Ruth and Orpah, both sons died a decade later.

Naomi loved Ruth and Orpah, but she had to return to Bethlehem, and she insisted that they stay in Moab when she did. Orpah obeyed Naomi, but Ruth would not leave her. Instead, she made a declaration to Naomi that many people recognize centuries later. She told Naomi, "Don't urge me to leave you or to turn back from you. Where you go I will go, and where you stay I will stay. Your people will be my people and your God my God. Where you die I will die, and there I will be buried. May the Lord deal with me, be it ever so severely, if even death separates you and me." (Ruth 1:16-17, NIV) Ruth was determined that nothing was going to separate her from Naomi or her God.

When Ruth and Naomi arrived in Bethlehem, they had no food, no shelter, and no one to care for them. They were poor, destitute, and at the mercy of those who would give alms to them. A foreigner and a widow, Ruth remained determined to take care of herself and her mother-in-law, so she decided to go out to glean, or gather, what was left in the fields (Ruth 2). Ruth ended up in the field of Boaz, a very rich, God-fearing man who was also a relative of Naomi's deceased husband. When Boaz saw Ruth in the field, he was so impressed by her devotion and commitment he told his workers to leave more harvest behind for Ruth to gather. He also introduced himself to Ruth and instructed her not to go into any other field so she would be safe.

When Ruth arrived home with an abundance of barley and food, she told Naomi what had happened, and

Naomi revealed that Boaz was a kinsman-redeemer for their family. Then Naomi, in her desire to find a home for Ruth, instructed Ruth to clean herself up, put on perfume, throw on some nice clothes, and follow her instructions on how to approach Boaz with their need. I love Ruth's response. "I will do whatever you say," (Ruth 3:5, NIV)

Like Ruth, I was obedient to the mentorship and coaching that I received. When I first met with my mentor, I was doing inventory work, going from one grocery or clothing store to another counting all the inventory at the different stores. I compiled the data and printed out a report to give to each of the store managers. It was good work, but my mentor saw that I could do more and *be* more.

I was receptive to every single instruction given to me, and within three years, I began working at the technology organization I am with today. I have seen myself grow by leaps and bounds since then. Every year, I have received a promotion, and I believe that is because of my willingness to listen to the wisdom of my mentor. Following the instructions of God, given through my mentor, has allowed me to come to a place of promise and into a season where God is truly blessing me.

I thought of Naomi's directives to Ruth when I started working at the technology company. My mentor, in an effort to help me sustain my position and receive promotion in the future, advised me to reexamine how I presented myself, particularly how I dressed. Specifically, she told me that I needed to dress for the job I wanted, not the one I had. Once I changed my mindset to view how

I could present myself differently, it began to open up opportunities in the organization for advancement.

Ruth had a choice. She could have done things her way or the way Naomi instructed. As told in Ruth 3-4, she decided to submit herself to Naomi's direction and leadership. This had a profound effect on Boaz. Boaz purchased land from Elimelech's inheritance to provide for Ruth and Naomi. Even more, he became Ruth's husband, they loved one another, and they had a child who would go on to become the grandfather of King David. Ruth's mentor, Naomi, even helped them raise the child.

Thanks to Naomi, Ruth became a person of great strength and influence and a woman of virtue. Whatever challenges came her way, Ruth was ready for them because of Naomi's continued influence in her life.

As we move up the corporate ladder, the type of circumstances we deal with change. I always assume positive intent from others until proven otherwise. However, there was a situation where I was meeting with a certain group of people at work, and I realized that their motives weren't pure toward me or my team. They were trying instead to create a position for themselves in the company. They were doing what was best for them and attempting to use me for their benefit. Though they said, "We are a team, and we are in this together," their actions proved otherwise. They weren't very trustworthy.

I had a choice. I could have responded negatively toward them, only thinking and caring about myself, but my faith would not allow me to do that. Instead, I remembered who I am—and that God had called me to that position to be light in the midst of the darkness. I couldn't act toward them the way they acted toward me, so I had to trust God that, even in the midst of their wrongdoing against me, His justice would prevail. In the end, I attained the position they were seeking to fill. What they were hoping to gain fell through, and people started to see them for who they really were. I didn't have to speak negatively about them. The truth came to light on its own.

Ruth certainly made decisions in view of her circumstances. As a Moabite, she came from a place where the people did not believe in God. Yet Naomi had such an impact on her that Ruth decided on her own to deny all of Moab's false gods to follow the God of her husband and her mother-in-law. Naomi must have had a great influence on Ruth to cause her to love God so deeply—and Ruth inspires me to be a representation of God in the workplace, no matter what goes on. I will be someone that people can trust. Others will know that I will execute my tasks to the best of my abilities, and I will do them in an excellent way. My faith helps me to remain honorable and ethical so that the choices I make will be pleasing to God regardless of whether or not others like, or agree with, my decisions. As Jeremiah 17:7 says, "Blessed is the one who trusts in the Lord, whose confidence is in him." (NIV) If I operate from a trustworthy place, God will reward me and protect me from anyone who tries to get me to make a wrong decision.

As I continue to excel as a woman in the workplace, I will remain content through my faith by trusting and believing that, in God, all things work together for my good (Romans 8:28). That means that whatever is for me is *for* me. Other people can do what they do, but what God has for me, no one can take away from me. I continue to hone my crafts and improve my skills so that I can represent myself as someone who is marketable, teachable, and equipped for whatever position God wants me to have.

Through my mentor, I have learned that promotion doesn't come from people. Promotion comes from God. One of my biggest goals was to complete my bachelor's degree. My mentor always asked, "How many more years until you graduate?" For years, my response was, "I have one more year to go." That was because, at that time, the only degree I had was a degree in procrastination. I kept putting off going back to school. Finally, I took the step of faith to return to school because I knew that my degree would help me in ways skills alone could not. I trusted God to help me through it and provide for me. Not only did I complete my bachelor's degree at Northern Arizona University in Interdisciplinary Studies with an emphasis on Humanities in 2020, but I continued on from there to get a master's degree in Business Administration from the University of Illinois in 2022. Because of those degrees, I have been able to excel and grow within the organization where I work, and I know my future is limitless.

There's no doubt Ruth dealt with difficulties. Her very upbringing was hard because she was a Moabite. The people of Moab were pagans who didn't believe in God. They had ungodly customs and traditions. All of that polluted Ruth's thinking as she grew up, so she had to change her mindset to allow God to use her to impact His Kingdom. Likewise, I have to mind my thinking as I encounter difficulty at work. My first reaction is to argue and stick up for my team. I want to make sure they are being treated correctly. So, I have to really seek God in those types of situations. Since He is the one who placed me in that circumstance, I want to represent Him to the best of my ability when I respond. I also have to trust and believe God will give me the solution that is honorable for me and for others while bringing Him the glory.

One thing that has helped me is to celebrate my leaders when things are going well. Everyone wants to hear words of affirmation and encouragement, so I am quite intentional about letting my boss know when there are wins within our group and our organization and to recognize his or her role in those victories. I also share feedback from my team with my leaders and compliment them when meetings go well. I give them encouragement about the things they implement and what they want to see happen as a result, and I point out the positive outcomes that have occurred because of their leadership.

Of course, when dealing with leadership, there are times when things don't quite go the way I thought they would. When I was first starting in my tech company job, my boss was getting ready to transition to a new position—and I really thought that I would be the one to replace her. I was doing a really good job. I was outperforming my peers.

Then I talked to my mentor about the transition, how I was being considered to fill the position, and how much I thought I deserved the opportunity. She told me she had been praying and that God told her that it was a "not yet" season for me. I wouldn't be the one to get that position. I could have been angry, but I had enough faith and trust in God to listen to what she said and wait to see what happened next.

She was absolutely correct. Not only was somebody else chosen for that position, but the company called on me to train my new boss. I could have been upset. Instead, I trained that person to the best of my ability. Within a few months, a different position opened up in a different department with more room for professional growth and future promotion, and I was able to take it. I had to trust that what God had in store for me was mine and that it was worth the wait.

Ruth had to trust that what God had for her was hers. When she was gleaning in the field, a lot of things could have happened differently, but Boaz told the members of his household to honor her, not touch her, and even to leave behind extra bundles of grain for her. Boaz saw the good—the God—in Ruth, and he believed in her. I, likewise, believe people see something different about me in the marketplace because of what God sees in me. He sees my hard work, my integrity, and my moral character, and those around me see that same fiber within me. I listened to God, followed His plan, went at His speed, and He promoted me. This happened because I listened to my mentor the same way Ruth listened to Naomi. She didn't tell Naomi, "Go and sit down. I don't want to do that. I'll handle this myself." Ruth honored her mentor completely, and God quickly took Ruth from gleaning the fields to owning them as Boaz's wife.

That made an indelible impression on my heart and showed me that I should honor my mentor and respond to her advice in the same way. Through my mentorship, it is always at the forefront of my mind that when things seem to be going bad or differently than I thought, I am to give them over to God. When things are going well, I am to give them over to God, too. I make sure that I give thanks in all things. I realize that every single promotion, every single successful project, every single elevation, and every single good report is because of God, and I give Him the glory for everything that is done.

The favorite thing my mentor tells me is to "keep my head down and color." I can so easily picture a child sitting at a desk, concentrating, getting out all those crayons, and being creative and inventive, but keeping her head down and her eyes on task, not getting ahead of herself or too full of herself. My mentor's statement is a call to humility. When I am on top and everything is going well, I need to keep my head down, color, and stay in a place of humility, realizing that I am where I am because of God.

Because of that, I am positioned and willing to help others understand what they are facing and make sure they are doing their job to the best of their ability and with humility. If I can help another person work through their challenges and be able to get to the place God has called them to be, I am ready to do it. In fact, the best thing I've ever learned is the importance of developing relationships with your mentors, those who have been where you are going and see potential in you that you may not see in yourself. Then you can pull that potential out of yourself and grow into a place of fulfillment—and do the same for others. Naomi poured so much into Ruth to help her maximize her potential, and you can do the same for those you influence in your life, especially in the marketplace where you serve.

In the end, my measure of success is defined by two questions. Is God pleased with me? Am I operating in the realm He has called me to? If I can answer "yes" to those questions, then I am successful.

I believe there is a place that God calls you to be where no one else can operate except you—a place where there is no competition, where there is no one to fight with, and where you can just go and do what God has called you to do. You'll experience that when you see your job as an assignment from Him and recognize your need for mentorship. That is my faith strategy in the marketplace.

I'll never forget when the COVID-19 pandemic hit in early 2020. My entire department had to take a 10 percent pay cut. At the same time, my living expenses increased. The cost of rent went up. I was worried about how I was going to pay for everything, and to be honest, it was scary. I didn't know how it was going to happen.

That is when my faith kicked in. I realized God was the one who paid my rent. Even with the pay cut, not one day went by when I lacked anything. When others told me that once the company took my pay, they would never give it back, I declared to myself that I *was* going to get my pay back. The following year, 10 percent of my pay was returned with an increase in compensation!

It is all about my mindset. My job is not my source. It is not my provider. It is not my main thing. God is. I trust and believe that what is for me *is* for me. I don't have to fight for it or undercut anyone to have it. I don't have to be unethical or lie, cheat, and steal.

I just need to know that every single thing belongs to Him.

That is more than enough for me.

Je're Harmon currently resides in Tucson, Arizona, where she is a woman who loves to laugh, is full of energy, and has a genuinely great attitude. When people meet her, they are drawn instantly to her. Je're is Associate Pastor at New Trinity Temple Christian Methodist Church. A major aerospace and defense company employs her as a personnel clearance data analyst and logistics lead. As staff executive for Amanda Goodson Global, LLC, Je're continues to incorporate her love for technology, planning, and facilitating to enable longstanding partnerships with business, industry, and nonprofit organizations. Further, Je're aspires to help others develop through media arts and visioncasting. She believes her success is possible by God's grace, favor, and guidance. Je're aims to grow her capabilities to advance the Kingdom on earth!

Contact Je're at Harmon.Jere@gmail.com

5

Let His Light Shine

Dr. Nannette Wright

Esther

"Then the king extended the gold scepter to Esther and she arose and stood before him."

(Esther 8:4, NIV)

Faith, according to the Bible, is defined as the substance of things hoped for and the evidence of things not seen (Hebrews 11:1) or, more simply stated, confidence in what we hope for and assurance about what we do not see. But for me, the demonstration of my faith means being a magnet that draws people to me so they can ask, "Why are you so joyful, kind, and compassionate? How can you stay positive when everything is so messed up?" If others are led *to* me so I can witness, it's because of what they see *in* me—God's light, then *that* is faith in the marketplace.

It isn't shouting from the rooftops, "Hey, I'm a Christian. Let me pray for you right now." It is that subtle but powerful light God exhibits through His believers to others.

When I think of this kind of faith, the woman in the Bible that comes to mind is Esther. In just 10 chapters, her amazing story is told in the Old Testament, and it reads like a page-turning novel. There's plot and intrigue, action and peril, and an incredible ending that shows Esther's undaunting strength of character and God's undeniable providence. I love how God's providential power worked in her life and how He orchestrated every step. Actually, He was not only working in her life, but also in the lives of several others. There was her cousin, Mordecai, who raised her as his own; Haman, the enemy who was trying to destroy her people; and King Xerxes himself and all of his servants. God used each and every one of them to set Esther up to do what she needed to become queen of the Persian Empire, the most powerful nation in the world at that time and, more importantly, to save her people from extermination.

Esther was born in a period of captivity that had begun over 100 years prior, when her Hebrew ancestors disobeyed God. Therefore, her people were despised and treated with contempt, much like people of color are treated in today's society. Yet God provided for Esther by having Mordecai adopt her, and she trusted in her God. Not only was she lovely on the outside, but Esther possessed an inner attractiveness that gained her favor with everyone she met (Esther 2:9, 15). It is our inward faith and how we present ourselves to others that gives us favor as well.

The king chose Esther, she became queen, and he loved her deeply (Esther 2:17). But when she learned from Mordecai that her people faced genocide because of Haman's prejudice against them, Mordecai told her she was the only one who could save them. God had placed her as queen, he said, "for such a time as this." (Esther 4:14, NIV)

Esther knew she was going to need help, so she prayed and asked everyone to pray for her. When things get stressful in the workplace, that's what you have to do. You have to pray and ask people to pray for you. I try to live that way in every job assignment, reminding myself that maybe God put me in that situation for a reason. Esther was afraid in her situation. She knew that if she went to the king when she hadn't been summoned, he could kill her. But even in her fear, Esther knew the power of prayer. Esther courageously called for a three-day fast for all the Jewish people while she prepared to go to the king, proclaiming, "When this is done, I will go to the king, even though it is against the law. And if I perish, I perish." (Esther 4:16, NIV)

God knew that Haman was going to try to kill all of the Jews, so He arranged for Esther to have the king's ear. She knew she needed godly wisdom to accomplish her task. The book of Esther chapters 5-8 unveils the plan God gave her as a result of prayer and her faith in its outcome. That plan unraveled the plot against her people, rescued them from certain death, and kept her in the king's favor. Esther understood that her actions influenced a lot of people. When you are a woman of faith, wherever you are, God has arranged it. He has ordered all of your steps. When you feel lost or unsure what to do, pray for wisdom and expect God to give it to you. You have everything you need to complete your assignment. I do my best to remember this, knowing that as long as I'm praying, and my family and my church are praying for me, I can be bold enough to go and do what God has called me to do and not be afraid.

Just as Esther meticulously prepared for her assignment before King Xerxes, I prepared for my next role as a leader in the defense industry while I waited for opportunities to advance. I wanted to be a director in a major organization. For over 10 years, I kept applying for positions, but it never happened. I became quite discouraged. Finally, when I least expected it, an opportunity opened up—and I realized that the roles I had before becoming a director were preparation from God. All that time, God had me in training, teaching me what I needed to know for my next assignment. I am so glad God made me wait because without those previous experiences I would not have been prepared to do the role effectively.

Shortly after becoming a director, the company I worked for went through a big merger. I'd only been with the organization for a year when my boss, who was also my biggest advocate, decided to retire. I was scared because we were told everyone would have to reinterview for their jobs, and some people would be displaced.

A few days prior to my interview with my new manager, I prayed and spent time seeking God for wisdom and guidance, and I asked my friends and family to pray for me. From that, I came to the conclusion, "It is what it is. God is in control." This reminded me of Esther when she realized she had no choice but to go and speak to the king, and said, "If I perish, I perish." Just before I was supposed to go into the meeting, I decided to put together a quick presentation detailing the things I had observed as areas of improvement for the company. I did it all very quickly, and I couldn't believe how fast everything came together.

I went into his office, and as we started our conversation, I could tell he thought I was only capable of doing a very limited role. He was giving me a vibe that he already knew where he was going to put me. Then I gave my presentation. He said with a smile, "I thought you could only operate at this one level, but now I can see that you can definitely operate at an entirely different level."

Right after that, the COVID-19 pandemic hit, and we were all working remotely. I remember sitting in my living room in front of my computer thinking, *This is crazy. This is going to be a journey. This will be a good book when it's all over.* As we started conducting one videoconference session after another, I strived to listen intently to what was being said in the spirit, not just in the natural. I asked God to give me wisdom, knowledge, and understanding to hear and see the problems spiritually so that I could solve them naturally. God was faithful and gave me specific insight to a challenge where we needed more focus in the area of risk and opportunity management.

I presented it to my boss, the same manager I had interviewed with earlier, and he gave me an entire organization to run with over 80 people! I tried to help all my employees become the best versions of themselves—and it ended up being one of the best experiences of my life. I learned more about organizational budgets, staff training, and providing discipline and rewards for employees. I have used each one of these skills in every job I've had since then.

Since the pandemic, I'm much more diligent about starting my morning with prayer. I go into my prayer closet, literally my bedroom's walk-in closet, to pray. I may only be in there for 10 minutes, but it feels like my superpower is activated because I know I am stepping into God's presence. It's as though I'm Wonder Woman putting on my suit and bulletproof bracelets, ready for any challenge. I put on the anointing of the Holy Spirit from head to toe to make sure I can face whatever comes my way. Oh, what a privilege to talk to God, anytime, any day, and ask for His guidance.

One time, I was in a new position where I was trying to make a change to the culture of the organization. I wasn't sure how to best handle the situation, and I really wanted to make a positive difference, so I entered into daily prayer, asking God for wisdom. He always answered whether it was through a direct word to my spirit or an article He led me to find. Eventually, He brought me a well-respected mentor who poured decades of his wisdom into my situation. He provided me with nuggets of insight and challenged me to read key books to gain multiple new perspectives.

The biggest thing my mentor did was let me know that my ideas were not farfetched. They were just different from what people were used to hearing and, therefore, hard for some people to accept. He made me realize that when I feel passionate about something that I know will make things better, I should not give up and think my ideas are no good just because people don't respond like I feel they should. I simply have to figure out how to reframe my ideas to get people to buy-in. "You don't have to convince everyone," he said, "just convince the right one." I thought that was just like Esther as she convinced the right one, King Xerxes, to marry her as God orchestrated all of it in the background. In addition, Esther wisely sought wisdom from those closest to the king. I imagine she wasn't a big fan of marrying a man she didn't even know, but Esther did what was required. *Alright,* she thought. *I've got this whole year. I might as well go through the process and try my best.*

Esther started securing favor with a few key people. That's what happens when God lets us know He has us covered, even when we're on an assignment that we aren't really thrilled about. For a while, you might wonder why it happened, but you have to get over it and say, "I am here for a purpose. Let me live out my purpose, so that I can get through it and please God in the process." Whenever I am navigating a difficult time, I quote Psalm 37:23-24, which says, "The Lord makes firm the steps of the one who delights in him; though he may stumble, he will not fall, for the Lord upholds him with his hand." (NIV) I remember that the plans God has for me are to prosper me and not harm me, but to bring me to an expected end (Jeremiah 29:11). I have to repeat His Word out loud (I have to hear it in the natural) so that my inner voice can receive it, know it is true, and help me navigate through whatever I'm facing.

An example of this was when I finished my Ph.D. in nuclear engineering in May 2000. I returned to my job after an extended leave of absence, and they no longer had any meaningful work for me. For about six months, I wondered what God was doing. Then I met Mr. Right (actually, Wright, pun intended). He lived in Philadelphia, I was in Texas, and I wanted to relocate to the Philadelphia area to be with him. However, I owed my company a lot of money since they had paid for me to go back to school for my doctoral degree. I had no idea how I could pay them back, find a new job in Pennsylvania, and hopefully marry the handsome and wonderful man I had met. I kept reminding myself of Jeremiah 29:11, and of the fact that God surely didn't allow me to complete my Ph.D. just to have no job satisfaction or life. Nearly a year after I met Mr. Wright, he told me his boss' sister-in-law worked for a big defense contractor. She volunteered to give my resume to her supervisor, who saw potential in me. Because of God's favor, I was able to repay my former employer for the Ph.D. with the bonus and other perks from my new job, move to Philadelphia with the new job, and become Mrs. Wright in November 2002.

As a leader in the marketplace, I understand that the higher one progresses in the chain of command, the more isolated and alone one becomes. It's harder to talk to others and divulge what is going on in different levels of the organization. So, whenever something goes well, I may send a coworker a text or an email saying, "Hey, that was really good," or "I'm so happy for you. That was great!" I encourage everyone, and even though I don't know exactly where they are in their faith, I tell them, "I'm praying for you." When I hear about a sickness or a big event in their lives, I slip it into normal conversation because it is important for them to know that prayer is powerful. Whether they believe in prayer or not, I think it gives them pause to wonder, "Hmm, I did feel a little different during this time. I wonder if there is a connection?" I also like to celebrate my coworkers, employees, and bosses. It is nice for people to hear a thank you and to know they are appreciated. Everyone needs encouragement, no matter what level of responsibility they hold.

Again, this is born out of my personal faith in God and my belief that all things work together for good through Him. I've seen that to be true over and over in my life and in the lives of others. My favorite saying is, "Sometimes the best deals you get in life are the ones you don't." So many times, I've been passed over for promotions and didn't get the interviews that I thought I'd get. I'd wonder what happened or why I wasn't good enough—but it wasn't God's timing yet. I look at where I am today, and some of the promotions and interviews that I didn't get, and realize I needed that different set of experiences to help me become the leader I am today. The delayed blessing (so I thought) was God's way of making sure I was equipped with everything I would need at just the right time.

Still, when you conduct yourself with all good intentions and integrity, it hurts when you are not recognized or rewarded for doing the right thing. It can even feel as though you are invisible or not part of the "in" crowd. However, you need to understand that God is watching everything that you do, and if you honor Him and represent Him in the marketplace, He will eventually promote you—and it will become easier to pray for those who haven't treated you right. This also allows you to keep your integrity intact and do what you are supposed to do knowing God will work out the rest.

Let me prove it. One time, during an annual performance review, my boss told me that, because my role was not as visible as others, he had to give me a less than satisfactory performance score. "You're not too bad," he said, "but I'm going to give you a bad performance review because somebody had to be in the bottom tier." I couldn't believe what I was hearing, but then it got even worse. My boss recommended I look for other opportunities in a different organization. I was more than a bit surprised. It looked and felt like a demotion, but I kept my composure and did not bad mouth him or anyone else at the company. As a result of that integrity, after a few short months God opened a door for a new job doing something I loved. It gave me visibility at the highest level of the corporation and provided the chance to travel internationally, which I had always dreamed of doing. The new job assignment also prepared me to rapidly learn new things and quickly decipher how to help organizations operate better.

I know how performance reviews work. Sadly, it is a game that everyone plays, but to get rated as not even meeting expectations? That hurt. I had worked so hard that year. Interestingly, my boss admitted that he couldn't sleep the night before our meeting, so I knew he felt guilty because it was not right. He even said he couldn't wait until I was in another position, and we could look back at this one day and have a good laugh about it. In the end, God turned it all around for the good (Genesis 50:20), and I am convinced that if I had murmured, complained, and badmouthed the situation, I would never have received the new opportunity, and God certainly would not have been glorified through me.

In order to continue to glorify God as a woman of faith in the marketplace, I stay in the now and try to thank God every day for what He is doing in my life. It doesn't have to be anything super big. In fact, I don't want to wait for the big things. I thank Him for all the little things because they really are big when you put them all together. When

I have to make a difficult phone call, I thank Him for giving me the words and wisdom to respond. When I have a presentation that I'm worried about, I thank Him that I have a job. When I have a concern about my kid, I thank Him that I have a kid.

I also thank Him for my health. Sometimes we don't value or miss something until it is gone. I have glaucoma, and in the fall of 2022, I had to have surgery on both eyes about six months apart. After the first surgery, there was a period when everything was a total blur. It looked like someone was holding a white piece of paper in front of my eyes during the day or a black piece of paper at night. I wondered if I was ever going to get my sight back. I was worried, but I decided to thank God for my one good eye. When I went in for my checkup, it turned out to be a minor issue, and my full vision returned—yet I still appreciate the reminder to praise Him for every little thing, even when I'm scared.

Esther had yet another great characteristic that I admire. She wasn't afraid to ask for help. When the women were to come before King Xerxes, they were sent through a time of purification so that they could look and be their best. These beauty treatments Esther received prior to going before the king consisted of 12 months of oils for massaging of the skin as well as perfumes and cosmetics (Esther 2:12). When it was Esther's turn to see the king, she didn't just pick what she wanted to wear. She asked the head servant what the king liked, so she would be best prepared to find favor with the king. Esther demonstrated a key principle we all need to understand; it's not always about you. Now that's wisdom!

In Esther's story, she also showed remarkable patience or, in the business world, political savvy. She first went to the king alone, then a second time at a banquet Haman attended (Esther 5). But it wasn't until her third time before the king that she revealed her true request (Esther 7). I believe she waited to hear from God. Remarkably, God worked behind the scenes after each delay to ensure His purposes for His people and Haman were set up to be fulfilled exactly as He wanted.

It's not easy to wait to hear from God. After working in one of my jobs for several years, I knew it was time to move on to something new. I had learned everything I could and was ready for my next challenge and promotion. Yet every time I thought an opportunity was there, the door slammed shut. Every night, I devoured all the employment websites looking for something new, but nothing happened. It became so routine, my son would see me on my phone, and he'd ask, "Mommy, are you looking for a new job," I was getting so discouraged. I'd tell him, "Yes, but there's nothing out there."

That's when, two years later, and seemingly out of nowhere, I received a request on LinkedIn from an executive with an opportunity that ended up leading to my dream job and a promotion. It proved once again that God only shows us the details of His plan when He knows we are ready to receive them. It's a hidden treasure that is revealed when the time is right.

From that and other experiences, I learned two valuable lessons about having faith in the marketplace: 1) Make sure you are prepared and surrounded by godly counsel, and 2) Don't be in a hurry. Let God lead you into your destiny. Promotion comes from God, not from people (Psalm 75:6-7). These lessons comfort me as I weigh the pressure of being in leadership and live a life of contentment through faith. I've always said that there's no such thing as work-life balance. All we can do is the best we can, and the way we do that is to continue to operate in faith and get wisdom from Him.

When I was younger, I wanted to be a vice-president or president at a major company, but the COVID-19 pandemic taught me that we could have nice clothes, shoes, cars, and all that stuff, but we didn't really need any of it. During the shutdown, there was nowhere to go. No one was looking at us except the people in our own homes. It really made me think about what was most important. My husband and my child were with me. We were safe. We were happy and content. God blessed me to keep working, but striving to get to the next level was no longer part of my thinking. I just needed to enjoy my family and not let my job consume me. My vocation was a part of me, but it didn't define my worth or take precedence in my life. As a result, I have learned to be calmer under pressure, knowing that wherever God wants to take me, it'll be in His timing, not mine. With every advancement in leadership comes more responsibility and greater consequences from the decisions I make. If I am not calm, everyone who works for me will not be calm, either. So, I'm learning to be more comfortable stepping out into my "uncomfortable zones" and trusting God, just like Esther did.

When I think of where I am today, all the things I get to do, and how I get to interact with so many wonderful people in my work, I am wowed by what God has done. I remember how it didn't seem like there was any way I was going to get here before that fateful LinkedIn message. As I left to go to my new job, people were like, "What?" How can someone progress from being in one position, doing okay but not really at the top level, to being at a much higher level at a different company? It made people pause and take notice. God recognized my efforts. I was able to tell people it was God, but I had to do some work, too. I did the preparation, I updated my resume, and I updated my LinkedIn profile. I learned as much as I could to prepare for whatever was going to come next. That's the key. We need to prepare for what's to come in spite of what we see in the moment.

One way we can do that is by being intentional in how we interact with those around us. My pastor, Bishop David G. Evans, once said in a sermon, "Every conversation is an interview." That stuck with me. No matter what you are talking about or where you are—the grocery store, at work, in a social function—you just never know how the person you are speaking with could connect you to other people or multiple opportunities. Mordecai was connected to Esther who was connected to King Xerxes, and look what happened? An entire group of people were saved from extinction. You just never know what doors could open when you have genuine conversations with others. That's why it is always so important to be kind, considerate, and thoughtful when dealing with people, getting to know them for who they are, *not* for what they can do for you.

This will also create opportunities to share your faith. I know for certain a big reason why God trusted and allowed me to complete my Ph.D. was so I could have conversations with intellectual people about Him, sharing faith analogies with them in a way they can understand. Many of my fellow students in the Ph.D. program believed they were intellectually brilliant and religion was for weak-minded people who had nothing else to rely on. For some, this perspective was born out of arrogance in their own abilities; for others, it was more a matter of the belief system they grew up with. Either way, I discovered they were more likely to listen to me because I was pursuing the degree. (Sad but true. It's just the way some people think.)

When I was almost finished with my doctorate, I was able to tell a few of my fellow students about God and how good He is. I used an experiment in quantum mechanics called Schrödinger's Cat Paradox to make my point. Schrödinger stated that if you place a theoretical cat and something that could kill the cat (in this case, a radioactive atom that has fifty-fifty chance of decaying and setting off a Geiger counter) in a box and seal it, there are two possible outcomes. If the Geiger counter goes off, a vial of poisonous gas is released, and the cat dies. If the material doesn't decay, the Geiger counter isn't set off, the poisonous gas isn't released, and the cat lives. However, the paradox states that we assume the cat is behaving like subatomic particles, so we cannot know for certain if the cat is dead or alive until the box is opened. Therefore, until you actually open the box and observe the cat, the cat is simultaneously both "dead and alive."[1] Sounds ridiculous, right? Yet quantum physics is based on this uncertainty that the particles exist in two states.

I postulated that the same principle applies in Christianity. We can't perform an experiment to measure that God is real—yet we know that the Father, Son, and

Holy Spirit all exist. If physicists accept that subatomic particles can exist in two states without seeing it, then why can't we believe that God is real? I could never have used a quantum physics concept to argue for God's existence if I hadn't studied that field, and my classmates definitely would not have listened to me if I wasn't seen by them as their intellectual equivalent. It just goes to show that God may place us in circumstances where it seems like we don't fit, yet we'll still manage to reach people and share His light as we take the opportunities presented to us.

That, in the end, is my measure of success. Did I shine my light today? Did I offer an encouraging word? Did I lift up someone who was down? At the end of the day, I want God to say, "Well done, my good and faithful servant."

I'm sure you do, too—so be sure to start your day with prayer, even if it's just for a few minutes. Let the Holy Spirit lead you each and every day. Give yourself grace when you fall down or feel weak in your faith. Reach out to your family and friends, and get back on the right path. We all fall down, but we all have to get up, too.

Never give up because you know your steps are ordered and God has a plan—then watch as others are led *to* Jesus because of what they see *in* you.

Dr. Nannette Wright was raised in the small town of Chillicothe, Ohio. She graduated from Purdue University with a bachelor's and master's degree in health physics and received her doctorate in mechanical engineering (nuclear engineering emphasis) from the University of Texas. Dr. Wright has worked for top defense contractors for over 20 years. She has demonstrated her commitment to identify and elevate the greatness each of us hold and bring it to the world. Nannette has served as Chairwoman of the New Jersey Educational Opportunity Fund and Urban Promise board member. She resides in New Jersey with her amazing husband and son.

Contact Nannette at https://www.linkedin.com/in/nannette-wright-phd-504a8442/

Notes

1   https://builtin.com/software-engineering-perspectives/schro-dingers-cat

6

The Devil Doesn't Always Wear Prada

Kim Dudley

Mary, the mother of Jesus

"'I am the Lord's servant,' Mary answered. 'May your word to me be fulfilled.' Then the angel left her."

(Luke 1:38, NIV)

 s a human resources (HR) professional with over 30 years of experience, I am that rare individual who actually sought out and intentionally pursued a career and postgraduate degree in HR. In other words, unlike many people working in that profession, I chose HR. It didn't pick me by default. Often, a company leader, upon realizing the importance of having an HR department, selects any random administrative person to run it, thinking, "Well, someone has to plan the holiday parties and terminate people."

Of course, human resources involves far more than that, and since I have always felt called to drive change, I was committed to creating and changing policies to make sure *all* employees were treated fairly. Even greater, I wanted to impact people's lives and leave an indelible impression on them and in the marketplace. In my mind, I am a "Super*HR*o" who influences the marketplace one industry at a time! Why not? Doesn't Matthew 19:26 (NIV) state that "with God all things are possible?"

It does—and thank goodness He is the Master with the master plan, the "author and finisher of our faith." (Hebrews 12:12, KJV). It was 35 years ago, exactly one month before I married my best friend and love of my life, that God called me to love and serve His people and be available for whatever assignments He deemed appropriate for me according to His will—including HR work.

You might be saying to yourself, "Wait. Isn't HR the policy police and the people who keep religion and politics out of the workplace?" I know I thought that! I questioned God, myself, and others who supported me in my profession. As a Christian in HR, I felt doomed and set up for failure! Why would God, my Abba Father, do this to me? Did I choose the wrong career? Did all of my hard work and degrees go to waste? At first, I was confused and did not know or understand how a woman chosen by God could be successful in my HR calling in the marketplace. It was like mixing oil and water!

That's when the struggles began, and they were my fault for creating tiny cracks for the enemy, Satan, to slip right into my faith space. I've learned that the effect of our tongues is equal to the pen of a ready writer. We will inherit what we proclaim! Because of my doubt, I often felt like quitting, and in one instance, I did, only to find myself in the same exact situation with a different employer. It was very easy for me back then, after a bad day at the office, to substitute reading God's Word with a glass of red wine, even with the understanding that such behavior didn't point to God and certainly was not the answer. I've never received revelation from a glass of merlot.

However, in the years that followed, through studying God's Word and surrounding myself with like-minded people of faith, I quickly learned my definition of faith in the marketplace: I had to put God's Word into action. I had to totally surrender to Him and trust Him unconditionally, despite the circumstances around me and what I was seeing with my natural eyes. I had to learn to operate more in the Spirit with the knowledge that He would prevail, through my obedience and communion with God and strong faith and prayer, and I would be victorious as well. I began to focus on and repeat Bible verses and affirmations to myself. I recall reciting 1 Corinthians 10:13 for nearly three months, which encouraged me that God would not give me more to bear than I was able to handle. That scripture, along with many others, filled my mental catalog and often supplemented personal theme music selections such as Yolanda Adams' "Victory."

Throughout these personal and professional challenges, I was often reminded of Mary, the mother of

Jesus. She faced many challenges and setbacks of her own in the Bible, yet she persevered and pressed forward to advance the Kingdom of God in her society with unwavering faith. I selected Mary as the woman I most identify with in Scripture because she birthed the ultimate intercessor, Jesus Christ, who is even now interceding for me, and all of us, before God the Father (Romans 8:34, Hebrews 7:25) as our advocate (1 John 2:1). As an HR professional, I intercede for the employees I represent and the company as a whole. Policy changes, and all of the myriad of responsibilities that fall within my purview, allow me to change the current narrative or create a new one that will have a positive impact on people in different ways and at many levels. Through my HR work, my other God-given assignments, my obedience to Him, and my faith, I am allowed to operate in an intercessor's mode as God sees fit to birth new things through me: strategies, solutions, and paths for others to grow, develop, and sometimes self-correct.

As I was writing this chapter, I told Je're Harmon, another author in this book, that I identified with Mary— and she immediately replied, "Oh, I can see that, not only for what you do in the marketplace, but for what you do in the church and how you have the ability to take nothing and make it into something." She mentioned the talents and gifts God gave me in decorative interior and exterior design work for homes and how I helped a pastor and others beautify their homes from the front door to the back door. "Your love and compassion are exuded through your design work." That shocked me. I never looked at what I did as a designer that way. It was actually very intimidating to consider, but as I stated earlier, all things are possible with God.

Mary inspires me through her obedience and her willingness to do as God directed despite what others said or thought. Just think of the simple fact that she was a virgin having a child. The angel Gabriel came to her and gave her that assignment (Luke 1:26-38), but how could she explain that? The answer was she couldn't, not beyond what Gabriel had told her. But that was enough for her. The fact that Mary set all that aside, despite the negative consequences she surely received from gossip, and did what God had called her to do is amazing. I resonate with her unwavering ability to surrender to God and be obedient.

God used Mary to teach me that we are employed by God—and my assignment in the marketplace is God's assignment for me, not my employer's. God is the ultimate employer who provides for both my financial security and my well-being.

The Devil Wears Prada is a 2006 motion picture in which Andrea Sachs (played by Anne Hathaway) is hired to work as the second assistant to powerful, sophisticated Miranda Priestly (Meryl Streep) and has to overcome the influences of her sometimes cruel boss who also wears Prada shoes. It was early in my career, when I worked for a very large multi-state healthcare company as their director of human resources, that my faith in Jesus was pressure tested when I had to deal with my own cruel supervisor. I reported to a male company executive who, later in my tenure, shared that he was a proud atheist. It seemed the more I tried to complete my assignment from God in that marketplace, the more the enemy showed up—and while, in this case, the devil *wasn't* wearing Prada, the boss still had to be dealt with.

I'll never forget the day I was scheduled to introduce some policy changes and benefits enhancements that would support the company's mission and provide better healthcare to our employees and their families during a very large executive meeting. I knew God had given me the solution I was going to present because I prayed and sought Him for it before acting on it.

That meeting ended up being the scene of the most embarrassing moment of my entire career. The changes I suggested called for an insignificant increase to one line item in my budget, and the atheist executive became enraged. His face turned as red as I imagined the devil's face would look as he stood up, glared, and pointed his finger at me. "This is unacceptable!" he yelled. "I did not authorize an increase to the budget! Anyone who's been paying attention for the past quarter clearly understands that!"

Caught completely by surprise, I tried very hard to maintain my composure, frantically searching through the collection of scriptures I had stored in my mind—but I was not successful. Instead, I let my emotions and frustrations show. My eyes got big as saucers and I shook my head in disbelief, thinking, *I don't believe he just did this.* I put my hands out in front of me as if to say, "What gives?" then sat silently for a moment as he finished his tirade. I replied, "Not a problem. I'll take care of it," then closed my laptop, gathered my belongings, and declared, "I am going to excuse myself from this meeting." I didn't ask to be excused. I just walked out.

After I sulked back to my office, I closed the door, got down on my knees, and asked God, "Why me? Why now?" Then I pleaded with the Lord to deliver me from my position and the atheist executive.

As soon as I stopped praying, crying, and whining, a small voice inside of me said, "No weapons formed against you shall prosper." It repeated, even louder, "NO WEAPON FORMED AGAINST YOU SHALL PROSPER!" Then the voice became softer and posed a question. "Don't you know that no weapon formed against you will prosper?"

I was astounded and ashamed that, after all God had bought me through and all that God had done for me, my great faith had diminished to the size of a mustard seed in less than an hour.

I repented on the spot, then immediately afterward wrote those words in bold letters on a sticky note and I stuck it on my laptop. I repeated that process at least a dozen times and strategically placed the other sticky notes in my desk drawers, in my briefcase, and even on the wall. I began to fast and pray for clarity and wisdom regarding God's assignment for me. I wanted to make sure that I was not operating out of bounds.

As suggested in my *The Devil Wears Prada* metaphor, the devil can show up in many forms and fashions, and I had learned to expect the unexpected when fighting against the enemy. But, like Mary, I also had an assignment to fulfill, and it was extremely important for me to stay obedient and birth the change God wanted for those employees in that company.

Once I received confirmation from God that I was working the correct assignment as an HR professional, I continued to fast and pray for protection and guidance. Within four days of that hostile meeting, a board member came by my office to ask if I was alright. He told me he actually supported my plan and my ideas and to not give up. As soon as he left, I praised God and thanked Him for sending me confirmation of what He had told me earlier. In the end, I revamped my plan a little, and two days before the next meeting, God did something remarkable. The atheist executive who had embarrassed and belittled me while trying to derail God's plan was asked to leave the company! Now, I wasn't excited that someone had lost their job, but I was overjoyed that God had removed the obstacle (my Miranda Priestly, to recall the motion picture analogy) who was trying to prevent me from being (like Andrea in the movie) my authentic self, so I could finish His work at that company. That person was eventually replaced by a God-fearing female leader who was anything but cruel. She supported me and my God-given assignments at that organization for the next four years, until I decided to leave the company to pursue a better opportunity in a different industry because my assignment there was done.

———

Since my "The Devil Doesn't Always Wear Prada" moment, I've had many other assignments over my career, and as an HR leader, I have been privileged to have insight into the lives of employees that have allowed me to pray for their personal and professional situations. Human resources is responsible for handling a company's many important functions, including the work lifecycle for every employee as well as their compensation and benefits. One very significant way God has given me opportunities to operate in my gifting is to be that soft, calming voice of peace and comfort to the family members of deceased employees. I help guide them through the life insurance claim and exit process (the *natural* part of my assignment) as well as pray for them to overcome their difficulties during their season of grief (the *supernatural* part of my assignment).

I once worked at a small company where one of the employees I knew well unexpectedly suffered a stroke and passed away. I recall his widow, Mrs. Dobson (not her actual name), sitting in my office sobbing uncontrollably as I offered a tissue and some tea. She had just lost the love of her life and the father of her children, and she didn't know where to go, what to do, or how she was going to survive. She was so broken and distraught as I placed my hand on her shoulder and gently repeated, "It's going to be okay." I gave her plenty of time to compose herself as best she could as I prepared the insurance claim and prayed silently for her and her family. About an hour into our meeting, I heard God prompt me to ask her if it was okay for me to keep her in my prayers, and without hesitation, I tenderly made the request.

Mrs. Dobson briefly stopped crying, looked me dead in the eyes, and said, "Wow. You have no idea what those words mean to me." She dabbed her cheek, then repeated herself.

"What do you mean?" I asked.

"When I leave this office," she replied, "my plan was to purchase a bunch of liquor and drink myself to death because I don't know how to go on without my husband. He and I would always pray for each other, and as he was dying, he asked me to keep praying and trusting in the Lord."

As my heart swelled with joy and pure amazement of God's perfect timing and will, His grace overwhelmed me because of what she didn't know: I had been scheduled to be out the office that day, but due to a conflict in my schedule, I had come in to work. I wasn't even supposed to be there.

Every time I look back on that situation, I realize I was meant to be employed by that company, I was meant to be at work that day, and I was meant to be there for Mrs. Dobson to process the life insurance and coordinate counseling sessions for her and her children as well as the employees who worked with and knew Mr. Dobson. Most of all, I was *meant* to be there to make that offer of prayer and hear her response. At the end of the meeting, Mrs. Dobson asked me to pray aloud with her, and I asked God, among other things, to give her strength and the peace to heal her broken heart. A few months later, I received a heartfelt thank you letter from Mrs. Dobson, sharing that her husband had told her how different and special the HR team was at his job compared to the other companies he had worked for—and how, now, she understood why.

That situation had absolutely everything to do with being faithful and obedient to God: listening to Him and acting on His behalf with love and showing the same grace and mercy that I receive over and over again every single minute of my life. In the Bible, 1 Corinthians 13:13 lists the virtues of faith, hope, and love, then says the greatest of those is love. God's greatest commandment in the New Testament is to love one another as He first loved us—and as a woman of faith in the marketplace, I strive to walk in that commandment every day as I unlock the door to my office and begin again to do my Father's work for the advancement of His Kingdom.

God has always wowed me in my career by giving me every single tool, resource, wisdom, and solution that I need for every single assignment, especially those outside of my comfort zone or way above my pay grade because they were beyond my knowledge base and experience. God has faithfully placed me in a position within organizations where I could discern when the company's financial stability was weak and volatile and the impact would have resulted in mass employee layoffs. God assigned me to pray for financial growth, revenue gain, and rebounds in the stock market for those organizations' investments so they could remain successful and thrive for the benefit of their workers and customers.

I have received so much good advice from others as a woman of faith, but the best piece of advice I have ever received came on December 15, 2019, shortly after my mother passed away and during yet another period of adversity in the workplace. The advice was from God. He told me, "Do not be weary in well doing. You will reap the harvest if you do not faint. Do not question what is happening. Go forth, and I will reposition you. You have an awesome testimony. Believe." Those words, the first portion of which quotes Galatians 6:9, remain pivotal to my life today—and I imagine God saying something similar to Mary after she was chosen as an unwed virgin to deliver the Savior of the world and whenever she grew weary during her pregnancy. The weight of being the earthly mother to Jesus Christ must've been heavy, yet she did not faint under its pressure.

As a queen in God's Kingdom and an ambassador for Christ in the marketplace, I measure my success on three things: 1) the fruits of my labor, shown when I see my prayers answered and God's solutions successfully implemented; 2) people for whom I've prayed sharing reports of good outcomes as a result of God moving in their lives because of my prayers; and 3) getting new assignments from God in the marketplace. Therefore, my faith strategy is to always be in communion with God so that, no matter how bad circumstances may seem or how Satan chooses to show up, I can remain faithful to utilize my personal rolodex of theme music and scriptures to honor and glorify God.

As women of faith, we will experience disappointments along the way personally and professionally. It could be an unskilled boss or members of your team who are poor performers in their job responsibilities. Whatever it is, know this simple truth: prayer works. Have faith in God and remember that He has the ability to move mountains, break chains, and make crooked places straight! (Isaiah 45:2) We all have plans for our lives. As a young woman, Mary surely did. She cherished her purity and her plans to marry Joseph, the love of her life, and she was ready to take on the roles of wife and mother, as most women did during her time. However, Mary wasn't aware that God had an entirely different blueprint for her and Joseph. She may have been disappointed when her plans were Divinely changed, but her faith and willingness to surrender her body—and her life—to God for the greater good of all mankind clearly set her apart. Mary's faith is even more profound when I consider how her initial disappointment must've been exacerbated years later when Jesus surrendered His life to His Father at the crucifixion. She witnessed for herself the unimaginable punishment and torture that her son (as God's Son) endured, yet her insurmountable faith in God helped her to overcome and endure.

Of course, when things are going well, it is equally important for us, as women of faith, to praise and worship God, and I do that regularly as I commune with Him.

My desire is to be in constant communication with God by prayerfully dispatching my angels to guide and guard my workday before I leave my house, trusting them to go to every single meeting I have scheduled as well as to guide and bless the words that come out of my mouth to bless the ears and hearts of the recipients. Dr. Amanda H. Goodson, my pastor and mentor, rightly says, "the effect of your tongue is equal to the pen of a ready writer." (From Psalm 45:1) I want everyone I communicate with to have a clear understanding of what God is saying to them, and I always want to act on God's accord, not my own, to be used as His vessel in my interactions with them and on behalf of others. I have faith and trust that God will never fail me, misguide me, or leave me.

While my biblical faith hero is Mary, my modern-day faith hero, aside from Dr. Goodson, was my mother. She was a product of the racial adversities in America in the 1950's and 1960's. Despite facing them on a daily basis, she relied on her strong faith in God to persevere. One of her favorite sayings was an adaption from Proverbs 3:5-6: "Trust and submit to only God, and He will do the rest." My mother impressed those words on the hearts of her husband and children every day of her life. Against the odds of her society, my mother was able to earn several degrees in her lifetime. She became a registered nurse for 26 years, taking care of and praying for patients in the emergency room. Her ability to draw strength from God, along with her determination to drive positive change in the marketplace during a 60-plus year career, made an indelible impression on me.

Her example keeps me motivated to drive positive change as I impact the lives of others—and to support that desire, I ask God to send me the type of employees I

want as colleagues or on my team: God-fearing, supportive people who meet the list of faith-driven attributes I
value. I do the same regarding board members and leaders
where I work. My faith strategy in the marketplace is to
try to always operate out of love, in obedience to 1 John
4:16. It says, "So we know and rely on the love God has
for us. God is love. Whoever lives in love lives in God, and
God in them." (NIV)

I strive to be patient and faithful, knowing that the
enemy will still come to kill, steal, destroy, and interfere
with God's assignment for me, but Jesus came that I may
have life more abundantly (John 10:10). That's why I
stand strong on the fact that I serve an omnipotent God
who is the Alpha and the Omega, the beginning and the
end (Revelation 22:13), the mighty warrior who will
always prevail, no matter what. I don't move unless God
tells me to move.

In Luke 1:46-48, Mary sang, "My soul glorifies the
Lord and my spirit rejoices in God my Savior, for he has
been mindful of the humble state of his servant. From
now on all generations will call me blessed, for the Mighty
One has done great things for me—holy is his name."
(NIV) May I humbly add to her praise a prayer of my own
and ask that you make it yours as well?

"God, You are greater than any person, job, or situation, and I want to honor You in everything I do. You
alone are worthy of my worship. Please remove all distractions or fears that keep me from staying focused on You
and completing my assignments today. God, thank You
for trusting and loving me, and for helping me put you
first in everything I think and do. In the mighty name of
Jesus, Amen."

Kim Dudley, MHRM, is certified as a human resources professional, corporate trainer, certified Hogan Trainer, and Six Sigma Blackbelt (HR) with over 20 years of diverse, executive level, HR leadership experience. A native of Chicago, Illinois, Kim and her husband relocated to Tucson, Arizona to support their children in their quests for postgraduate degrees in medicine and science, as well as to escape the brutal winters of the Midwest.

Kim has lent her HR expertise as an HR executive leader to both the public and private sectors in Tucson. In her current role at Southwest Gas Company, Kim is responsible for leading and managing several HR teams and initiatives for the company's Arizona division. Kim is also the founder and CEO of Soles For Souls Organization (solesforsoulsorg.org), a Tucson-based nonprofit whose mission is to provide new shoes to those who are in need in an effort to help mitigate sickness, and to provide hope and support opportunities for sustainability.

Contact Kim at kdudley@solesforsoulsorg.org

7

Unwavering Belief

Rev. Yolanda Jackson

Mary Magdalene

"Mary Magdalene went to the disciples with the news:
'I have seen the Lord!'"

(John 20:18, NIV)

aith in the marketplace is action. By faith, I understand that the universe was formed at God's command. That tells me that faith is in motion, and since I walk by faith and not by sight, I further understand how faith operates. Without works, it is dead (James 2:26)—so faith is something I need to practice with unwavering belief that it always produces good fruit.

I can't move in the marketplace and do what I've been sent to do without faith. It has been given to me as grace. My faith isn't something I could have worked for. It was a gift, entrusted to me, so that I can go into the marketplace and allow myself to be used by God for the benefit of others and for His glory.

To successfully exemplify and operate in this faith, I have to show up and make myself available. I don't do this alone. I show up with God to do whatever is required for that time and that situation. I am determined to take the light God has given me as I go, so others can see His great works through me. I am a carrier of hope to those who might be experiencing adversity, lack, disappointment, or pain. Therefore, I have to be a bold risk taker, so I can render aid as it is needed and come alongside others in thought, word, or deed. As I do, I have confidence in my faith, which allows me to be in that place for that moment. That confidence enables me to be effective.

As a nurse and as a leader, the woman in the Bible who inspires me the most is Mary Magdalene, who was freed by Jesus Christ from the mental and spiritual torment of being possessed by seven demons (Luke 8:2). I can somewhat relate to what she must've been going through because in June 2003, still new to my faith, I was delivered from a spirit of oppression.

When I experienced this radical transformation, it was a Sunday morning, and I was in church praying. I was experiencing fear, pain, and low self-esteem stemming from abuse that had led to mental anguish and much confusion. I had no one in my life who could speak to my hurt or to my situation. It was so bad, I felt as though the enemy of my soul wanted me to become mentally deranged.

During the prayer portion of the service, the pastor announced, "There is someone here today who wants to say something to the Lord." I was kneeling at the altar at the front of the church, and I was still there when he made that statement a second time. It was as if he had spoken it directly to me, and I knew I needed to respond.

I cried out in a loud voice, "Lord, forgive me for all my sins! You know I suffer daily. I thank you for grace, and I thank you for mercy, but where is your power?"

As soon as I spoke, it was as if Jesus Himself came down from Heaven, picked me up, and rocked me in His arms like a baby. I couldn't explain it! I cried and cried, but when I sensed that Jesus had set me down and was leaving, I cried out again and started reaching up into the air, trying to hold on. "Jesus, don't leave me here!"

I remained on the floor weeping until someone placed a white sheet over me. It was when I got up off the floor that I felt chains and shackles fall away from my body. I experienced the truth of John 8:36 that he who the Son sets free is free indeed. The Spirit of God then said to me, "Yolanda, I am calling you into the ministry. Will you accept my calling?" I gave a resounding, "Yes."

He said, "It is not going to be easy. Will you accept my calling?"

I again responded, "Yes."

He then said, "I have seen how you have stood against the giants, and I need people like you to serve in my Kingdom."

I received that calling in August 2003—and over two decades later, I'm still making a difference in people's lives, benefitting others with unwavering belief in the gift of faith God has given me.

I will always recall what God did for me that day just as Mary Magdalene remembered what Jesus did for her. I don't know if her situation was quite the same as mine, but I believe that she also suffered from a form of oppression. Oppression is defined as "mental pressure or distress," and I have learned more about it since I was delivered. I've also been busy serving God, with Mary Magdalene as my role model. After her own deliverance, she became a devout follower of God. She helped Christ and His disciples in any way she could and financially supported His ministry with them. Mary was also at the foot of the cross during Christ's crucifixion, and three days later, she was the first at the empty tomb and the first person to see Jesus after He had risen from the dead (Mark 16:9).

The scene that morning must've been incredible! It was still dark when Mary arrived at the tomb and saw the stone rolled away. Convinced someone had stolen Christ's body, she was distraught and perplexed. Mary Magdalene was still crying when she suddenly saw two angels in white seated where Jesus' body had been. Moments later, she turned around and saw a man standing before her. She thought he was the gardener.

That's when He said one word—her name—and she knew! It was Jesus! He had risen! Joy swept through her. Thrilled and amazed, Mary then went and told the disciples that she had seen the Lord (John 20:17-18). What an honor and privilege it must've been to be the first to see Him and to deliver the incredible news to His chosen ones.

I want to be like Mary Magdalene. I want to continue to learn everything I possibly can about who Christ is and what His purpose is for my life. I have encountered a lot of adversity in my life, but the one thing that has always carried me through is my faith.

I also believe Mary's faith is an encouragement to all women, especially those in ministry. Women are often marginalized, but God made it plain throughout the Bible that we are not substandard. Instead, we are to be influencers that share hope to a lost and dying world with authority and validation. Mary Magdalene is proof! The Lord entrusted the most important historical event of all time to her. She was the first to preach the message of Christ's resurrection!

———————

I served for 22 years in the nursing corps of the United States Army Reserves, and it was a remarkable experience! I joined in 1981 when I was 18 years old and attending Macon Junior College in Macon, Georgia. My older sister told me about the Reserves and how they would pay for college and that was inviting. But I knew I had to prepare for the rigors of physical fitness required to serve, I took a jogging class to learn to pace myself and breathe correctly. Then I signed up for the tuition assist program that fully paid for my college education. As my service skill, I chose to be an operating room technician. I underwent eight weeks of basic training at Fort Jackson, South Carolina during which I was a squad leader and graduated with an outstanding performance certificate.

Near the close of my term of service, I began struggling with weight compliance. I'd just had my children, I was older, and I was facing a lot of life pressures and stressors. As a result, I was being considered for discharge. I didn't possess the required records from when I went into the

Reserves, and without them, I could not prove my time of service. I was told the only way I could get that proof from the Army was if I had lost the records in a natural disaster or a fire. I was frightened that I wouldn't get my benefits.

The first time I called the Defense Finance and Accounting Service in Indianapolis, Indiana, I was denied access to the records—but the Holy Spirit prompted me to call again. I did, explained once more what was going on, and the person on the other end sent me everything I needed to prove my 22 years of service and receive my full retirement benefits.

That was a pressure test, and it served as a measuring device for my faith. Every time something comes up that doesn't quite go the in the direction I would like it to go, God reminds me that, since He saw me through that time in my life, He will see me through the rest, and I should never doubt who God is. That is unwavering belief. One thing I have discerned about Mary Magdalene's character was her ability to keep her eyes on the Lord, the author and perfector of our faith, who, "for the joy set before him he endured the cross, scorning its shame, and sat down at the right hand of the throne of God." (Hebrews 12:2) I desire to do the same.

Over the last 17 years, I have cared for elderly people with mild mental or physical disabilities. I open my home, and it becomes their home. I don't think of my things as being mine alone. I share what I have. It helps me not to be selfish, and God sends people into my path to encourage me and speak Bible scriptures to delight my heart. I had just started my business in 2006 and was preparing my home to receive my first clients when I found myself downcast and a bit lonely in heart. For so long, I had gone out into the workforce, but now I had been called away from that. It was quite an adjustment. Despondent, I walked up the street to a garage sale. The lady overseeing the sale was a real estate agent who also happened to flip houses, and she had some things I could use for my business, should it ever grow to that capacity. I bought a few items at the sale and was returning home when I came across another woman. She declared, "Isn't this a beautiful day that the Lord has made?"

I replied that it was, and as I continued home, I felt perked up. I went inside—and the next thing I knew, my husband was asking me to come to the front door. The woman was there, and she had been talking to him about the Lord. She had also been to the garage sale I had visited earlier, and she showed me what she got: a cake mold shaped like a lamb that she was going to use to make her little grandson a birthday cake.

Then she introduced her companions. "These are my two dogs, Goodness and Mercy, which shall follow you all the days of your life."

I was stunned. She had a lamb-shaped cake mold and two dogs named Goodness and Mercy. The parallels with the Bible were undeniable. As she left, the lady told my husband and me that she lived in an apartment "right up the hill" from us. But when I walked to the end of the street, there was no hill and there were no apartments.

I am convinced God sent that lady that day with a word just for me.

Goodness and mercy would follow me all the days of my life (Psalm 23:6).

Since that truly beautiful day, I have continued to learn that I can't rely on myself to strive forward and remain content. I must rely on God, "For I know the plans I have for you," declares the Lord, "plans to prosper you and

not to harm you, plans to give you hope and a future."
(Jeremiah 29:11) My hope and my future are connected
to Him. Whatever I do is because it's what He wants me
to do. I might want to do something, but I always ask, "Is
that what God wants?"

———————

As I consider how my faith in the marketplace has helped
me to grow in my calling to ministry and in my capabilities as a caregiver, I remember how the Lord told me to
develop a "posture of prayer." I didn't quite know what
that meant at first, but whenever the Holy Spirit speaks
to me, I go into investigative mode. I study as much as I
can about whatever He has told me. As I do that, I have
come to understand that there is an anointing on my life
to bless other people through my prayer life to give them
hope and encouragement in their faith. Just as I believe
Mary Magdalene had the character to stay focused on her
assignment to attend to the things of Jesus—His ministry,
the carrying forth of the message, and the finances of that
ministry—I also don't look to the left or to the right. I
keep my eyes on Jesus, for that was how she was successful
at being a follower of God. Mary Magdalene was a strong
and faithful support to Jesus. She was one of the few who
did not flee when He was arrested and suffering.

Likewise, when I experience difficult times and life feels
unfair, I can't be swayed by injustices. I can't be perturbed.
In the military, there is always a mission. Sometimes, it
is top secret. But our mission as people of faith in the
marketplace has been determined by God, and there is
nothing secret about it. It's called the Great Commission,
and it has been proclaimed by Jesus Himself. "Go and

make disciples of all nations, baptizing them in the name of the Father and of the Son and of the Holy Spirit, and teaching them to obey everything I have commanded you." (Matthew 28:18-19) There are people in the world who are lost, dying, and sick who need deliverance, healing, or just a kind word. That's my mission: that whatever a person's needs are at that moment, they will be met—not by me, but by the one who sent me, Jesus.

My first clinical rotation in nursing school was at an adult care home, and it was there that I developed a deep-seated, heartfelt passion for that community. I have a special place in my heart for the elderly. They are great storytellers of their lives, and as they interacted with one another, I saw that they were innocent yet challenged as aging vessels. Much later, when I became a caregiver, the very first client who came into my home had been diagnosed with pancreatic cancer. He wasn't expected to live very long. As I rendered care and medication, I was always praying for him. About six months later, incredibly, he was healed. The cancer vanished, he no longer needed to be under my care, and he left to live on his own. I was just being a caregiver, but I believe God used that situation to show me He was the healer. God always wants me to know His presence and His abilities.

As I continue to care for elderly people with mild mental or physical disabilities, I receive encouragement and inspiration from the leaders in my life, particularly those at church. I am thankful for them. I celebrate them as I obey the directives of Hebrews 13:17 to have confidence in and submit to my leaders, for they keep watch over me as those who must give an account to God for their actions. At the same time, whenever disappointments have come my way, my faith has helped me through it because, like Mary Magdalene, I remained focused and intentional about my relationship with God. During the COVID-19 pandemic, I had to do just that when I unexpectedly found out that I was not being reassigned to the church that I was pastoring at the time. I was attending an online annual conference of the Christian Methodist Episcopal Church in 2021 when the bishop who makes or confirms the pastoral appointments called my name, said, "not there," and then called the name of the person who was going to replace me as pastor of the church. It was concerning and unjust, and I felt I was mishandled by church leadership. Nevertheless, I was never told what brought on the decision.

Yet, even as I grieved the loss and dealt with my disappointment over how it happened, I moved forward with unwavering belief and in gratitude to the Lord. In 2023, I was with a group of spiritual leaders in my community called Preacher's Peace who meet every Wednesday. I lead a Bible study and answer invitations to preach. I know the truth of Psalm 34:19. "Many are the afflictions of the righteous, but the Lord delivers him out of them all." (ESV) I remember that the Lord is with me. It doesn't matter what challenge life may bring. If God is for us, then who can be against us? (Romans 8:31) If you don't get the promotion, you still have Jesus. Not even betrayal can separate you from the love of God in Christ Jesus (Romans 8:38-39). You can trust that He is the same today, yesterday, and forevermore (Hebrews 13:8).

———————

Worship and adoration of God are hallmarks of my faith in the marketplace. His goodness is incomprehensible.

God has supernaturally caused me to experience the manifestation of His goodness in my family, business, ministry, finance, and community. Galatians 6:9 exhorts, "And let us not grow weary of doing good, for in due season we will reap, if we do not give up" (ESV) I know that it is through the empowerment and embodiment of Christ, that is in me and comes from heaven, that others around me will experience God's love and light, resulting in healing, deliverance, and wholeness of life with restoration.

I recall how much I praised God as He wowed me at an Easter sunrise service in 2005. I had received my call to preach, and my pastor gave me the opportunity to do so at the service. I had never preached before, and I didn't know anything about it. No one had ever tried to teach me how it was done, but the Bible says the Holy Spirit will teach us whatever God wants us to know. As John 6:44-45 says, "No one can come to me unless the Father who sent me draws them, and I will raise them up at the last day. It is written in the Prophets: 'They will all be taught by God.' Everyone who has heard the Father and learned from him comes to me." (NIV) I watched a lot of the Trinity Broadcasting Network, and I tried to learn by picking up strategies from great preachers such as T.D. Jakes. I was still preparing when a friend who I had invited to the service recommended that I not read my sermon notes. He said I should just open my mouth and speak.

Fortified with that advice, I asked one of my friends who could play guitar and sing really well to open the service, and it was very beautiful. Then, all of a sudden, the glory of God fell, I put my notes away, and opened my mouth—and I had a Jeremiah 1:9 experience. "Then the Lord put forth His hand and touched my mouth, and the Lord said to me: 'Behold, I have put My words in your mouth.'" (NKJV) I had never preached before, but the Holy Spirit spoke through me, and the sermon that followed came directly out of Paul's great teaching about righteousness and accountability from Romans 3:9-18. I saw a lady shout! I'd never seen her do that in all the times I'd seen her in church. Then the pastor shouted. The entire congregation was in awe of the presence of God as the Holy Spirit's anointing fell on them. It was so exciting!

God has taught me so many important lessons in ministry and in life that I believe you can use as you express and maintain your faith in the marketplace. Nurture your spirit with prayer, fasting, and Scripture. Exclude the worldly entrance of outside distractions like news and gossip so that you enable your spirit to be sensitive to God's presence and direction, and you can clearly hear your purpose. See your pain, trials, and suffering as being for the testing of your faith, for "these trials will show that your faith is genuine. It is being tested as fire tests and purifies gold—though your faith is far more precious than mere gold. So when your faith remains strong through many trials, it will bring you much praise and glory and honor on the day when Jesus Christ is revealed to the whole world." (1 Peter 1:7, NLT) This Bible verse also encourages me. "But he knows the way that I take; when he has tested me, I will come forth as gold." (Job 23:10, NIV)

You are an ambassador for Jesus Christ (2 Corinthians 5:20), which means you represent and advertise the gifts that have been handed down to you, so He can use the abilities He has entrusted to you to serve others and showcase God's talent in the earth realm. First Corinthians 6:19 exhorts, "Do you not know that your body is a temple of the Holy Spirit who is within you, whom you have [received as a gift] from God, and that you are not your own [property]?" (AMP) As a nurse, it is my duty and obligation to serve others. With the aging population I serve in my care facility, I use my hands to serve, my feet to carry the service, and my voice to evoke a smile or calm a restless spirit. What I do comes from God. He created each one of the people I serve, He knows what they need, and He allows it to be rendered through me, a broken earthly vessel. What encourages me and warms my heart the most is how they light up when I enter a room after being out attending to other matters. When they can't speak, their eyes sparkle or they wave a hand. Others will say, "There you are! I was wondering where you were. I've been missing you!" That is priceless, and it always reminds me of the truth of 1 Corinthians 6:20. "You were bought with a price [you were actually purchased with the precious blood of Jesus and made His own]. So then, honor and glorify God with your body." (AMP)

Finally, I encourage you to "seek first the kingdom of God and His righteousness" (Matthew 6:33, NJKV) and live by this quote from the incomparable Martin Luther King, Jr. "To be a Christian without prayer is no more possible than to be alive without breathing." Focus on the mission God has given you, and do not become easily distracted by what is going on all around you. Have boldness and be confident to take risks, for you have the backing of the Kingdom of God! Be intentional, deliberate, and purposeful—and you are sure to succeed in practicing your faith with unwavering belief.

Rev. Yolanda Jackson completed 22 years of service and retired as a major in the United States Army Reserves Army Nurse Corp. The beauty of being a reservist and a civilian was the ability she had in serving God, her country, and her community. During her last tour of duty, Rev. Jackson heard the voice of God. She told everyone she had been called into the ministry! As an ordained minister, she has served and participated in many spiritual activities, workshops, and conferences. Rev. Jackson has served as Pastor of St. Paul Evangelical CME Church and First CME Church, both in Anchorage, Alaska.

She has continued her nursing career as an administrator/owner/operator of Guiding Light Assisted Living Home in Eagle River, Alaska. She has been a surgical operating room nurse at Creekside Surgery Center for 12 years. She works for Providence Hospital as a hospice on-call nurse. Rev. Jackson has been married for 25 years to the father of her two young adult children, Joshua and Wilanda.

Contact Yolanda at guidinglight61@gmail.comv

8

Giving Back—Giving Hope

Rev. DeLeesa Meashintubby

Lydia

"One of those listening was a woman from the city of Thyatira named Lydia, a dealer in purple cloth."

(Acts 16:14, NIV)

Huntington, Arkansas is a tiny, tree-peppered town of a few hundred people with a state highway running straight through it. If you weren't paying attention as you drove, you'd miss it entirely—but it was there, in that humble little place, that my parents first taught me to give back, no matter what.

Today, as executive director of a non-profit medical clinic, Volunteers In Medicine of Lane County, in Eugene, Oregon, I am able to live out that foundational teaching, confident that God has placed me on a path and that I will succeed. Why? I keep the faith that God will use me as a tool to market the clinic and to let the world know that they are not only giving money to a medical organization, but they are also giving back and being Good Samaritans by taking care of their neighbors and giving them hope.

There was a woman in the Bible who was also noted for giving back and giving hope—and I resonate strongly with her in my role as a woman of faith in the marketplace. Her name was Lydia, and based on how she earned her living, she was either unmarried or a widow. She had traveled from her hometown of Thyatira to the Roman colony of Philippi as a cloth dealer (Acts 16:14), and her quality textiles were surely in high demand. Already a worshiper of God, Lydia was introduced there to Paul. God opened her heart to his message, and she and her household, possibly containing children and servants, were baptized.

But that's not all that happened. Lydia immediately wanted to serve God, so she boldly offered her home to Paul, Silas, and Timothy (Acts 16:15, 40). She was determined to help those who labored for Christ. Biblical scholars believe that her home became a regular meeting place for believers and perhaps the very birthplace of the Philippian church.

In her brief story, it is clear to me that Lydia did an honest job helping her household, the community, and the economy. As a merchant, she provided for those in her home as well as for others. There's also no doubt that

Lydia influenced others as she gave them hope in God. She followed the path God set for her, and she helped support the new Christian church to keep it progressing and see it multiply throughout the world. Along the way, Lydia never allowed her work or other obligations to get in the way of her commitment to her faith in God.

I face much the same challenge to keep work and faith in balance as Lydia did. In addition to being an executive director, I pastor St. Mark Christian Methodist Episcopal Church. It is the oldest African American church in Eugene, and there were only three people in attendance when I took over in 2021. By May 2023, we had 57 members, the majority of which were white, followed by African American and then Hispanic. God has used me to grow the Christian church in my community, and I am proud of its diversity. I love every group of people, no matter their color, race, or ethnicity. We see each other's hearts, not our skin.

I experienced a bit of racism, though I was too ignorant to know it, when I was a child. I thought it was normal that I lived on this side and others lived on that side. Yet I still had friends, and all of them were white except for my cousins that I hung out with on the weekends. So, even then, God gave me a heart for all people that I have carried over into my adult life. I believe Lydia was the same way. She accepted everyone she encountered as a merchant in the marketplace and as a host for the believers who gathered at her home.

The Bible does not reveal if Lydia experienced difficulties in her business dealings with vendors or customers, but I can imagine that she did—and her faith in God surely carried her through them. My faith certainly displayed itself when I took over as executive director at the medical clinic in 2012. I had been there as front office coordinator, volunteer coordinator, and senior operations officer and clinic manager since it opened in 2001, but when I became the executive director, the organization was running at a deficit. In response, I started going through staffing, identifying redundancies, and cutting worker's hours or laying people off. I did not like doing this because I had been a peer with many of those workers and many of them were friends.

But our mission at the clinic was to let the public know that we were doing our due diligence, and that had to be my priority as executive director. We ended up saving over $105,000, and at a non-profit, that is a huge amount of money. I made some enemies, and there were others who just didn't understand. These workers weren't just there to take care of the underserved in the community. It was a paycheck to them. They needed the income for themselves and their families. That's what made me feel so bad about what I had to do—but that's where the faithfulness of God came in. He told me to do it. It was my job to obey Him.

Lydia certainly obeyed God. There was just something in Lydia's life that caused her whole family to know God, and that caused them to want to serve Him. I recall, when my husband, Norval, saw my faith and how I was willing to step out, saying, "God told me I have to do this," he started to believe in God because He saw the Lord manifesting Himself in my life. It happened one day in 2019 when I was praying in my bedroom. He could hear me from the living room, and when I came out to go to the kitchen, he said, "I now have to believe in what you are believing in because I see what is happening to your life." He saw that God was real in my life, and He wanted it for himself.

Today, he teams with me at our church. I call him the chief cook and bottle washer, and he does all the important little things so that I can study and stay in the Word of God and not have to deal with things that would take away my focus. I can also attend to specific needs of the congregation who need counsel and take care of church services and operations. He tells me, "You were called to do this. I wasn't. I was called to help you." Norval is amazing!

Throughout my career, whenever pressure came upon me, it usually meant it was time to finish the present assignment and move to the next level in my personal and professional development. God tells me when He knows I'm strong enough to make that move, and He empowers me to go to a different place where I can learn from others. When this happens, I strive to go to people who are brighter, smarter, and stronger than me because that's how I discover new things. After all, if I am the smartest one in the room, I can't grow. After a while, I will be old and stagnant, and I'll want to stretch out. At first, I feel like the dumbest tool in the shed, but as I learn, that changes, and my confidence grows. God has given me discernment to know who I need to learn from the most and who is best for me. I also realize that as I move to the next level, I make room for somebody else to come in and take my place, and I don't want to be a barrier to somebody else's blessing.

Of course, as I've made those moves, I've had to deal with times when I didn't get the recognition I should've. In 2004, when I served the clinic as front office coordinator, I came up with an idea to give cards to the people at our free clinic that stated the start and end dates of their eligibility. They would have to reapply for the cards every six months. I saw it as a good way to remind our patients when it was time to rescreen and to establish more consistency for us as an organization. The board of directors agreed and thought it was a great plan—but they were led to believe the business director, not me, had originated the idea. I didn't get the credit I rightfully deserved.

I thought, *Hmm. Maybe that's what my role is, to make her look good.* I also recalled the scripture from Proverbs 18:16 that said, "A gift opens the way and ushers the giver into the presence of the great." As the years progressed, my gifts indeed started opening the way. I wanted to hide in the background, and God kept pulling me to the front.

An unexpected benefit of that truth came in January 2023 when I received an award recognizing me as, "First Citizen of Eugene." Each year, the Eugene, Oregon Chamber of Commerce picks someone who does a lot for the community to be the citizen of the year. The award is given annually to an individual who has made notable contributions to the community through business and community service efforts. A panel of former First Citizen honorees selected me, and I think I was the first or second African American to get the award. When I was contacted about receiving the award, I was told the chamber wanted me to come to a ceremony and dinner where they would announce the honor and I would speak to attendees about the underserved population in Eugene.

There it was! I had gone from being in the background to a place where God had me out in front of over 600 people. That was a *lot* of people for me, and it let me know that God saw me. However, at first I wondered if my professional life was almost over. Then a gentleman, who had received the same honor a few years earlier, came to me during the event and said, "Don't you dare think this is the end of what you are doing. There is still more to come." Then he turned and walked away. I hadn't expressed that out loud to anybody.

Nearly six months later, another gentleman sent me an email telling me that he had been thinking about my speech, and he just had to send a video link of the speech to me. It was the first time I had seen the speech, and as Norval and I watched it that night, we just thought it had to be God. The words were prophetic, not anything I saw in myself, and it was a timely message for the season we were in right then. I spoke about "the dash" between two dates: the day we are born and the day we die. People may not remember those dates, I said, but they will remember what you did during the dash. Prophetically speaking, we are born and we will die, but it's what we do in between that matters. This is the time to make it count. That gives us hope!

God wowed me as I was recognized as the First Citizen of Eugene. I didn't even know such a thing existed. I had been sick that day, and I didn't know if I could show up for the event. But I said, "Okay, God, it's you and me. We are going to have to do this." I went in with nothing prepared to say, but He gave me words that brought new life to those who were there. It was so refreshing. I even had a gentleman, an older, white man, come to me afterward and say, "You've made me rethink woman preachers." It was incredible how God took a message about leaving a legacy in life and spoke to that individual about something completely different but uniquely significant to him.

Just because we are doing something now doesn't mean God doesn't have another page to turn for something else to happen. It makes me think about Lydia. She must've had a thought in her mind about being a cloth dealer that developed into a dream and then a plan that she had to execute. In order to get where she was, Lydia had to come out of hiding and into the foreground. She had to trust the Lord that He had more for her to do. She inspires me, too, because she lived and worked as a successful merchant in a culture where women weren't seen as being equal to men. I'm sure she didn't get a lot of, "Way to go, Lydia!" She had to be comfortable doing what she was doing without questioning why no one was telling her she was doing a good job. The blessing of the Lord and His acknowledgement was her reward.

There have been moments when I've experienced difficult times in the workplace that I have forgotten who I was really working for. I'd want to receive my, "Good job, DeLeesa!" But I've discovered God sometimes needs to snap our suspenders and say, "Who are you truly doing this for?" That's when I have gone back to the basics to find God working in the midst of it. Volunteers In Medicine of Lane County is a free clinic for the underserved populations of Eugene, and there are those in the community who donate to the clinic for the recognition and status they receive as much as, or more than, to help the people we serve. Sometimes I've thought, *Oh, this person wants to have dinner with me. I've got to do this and that—dress a certain way or talk a certain way—for them.* It was almost changing me into someone that I wasn't. Then God said to me, "Who are you doing this for, DeLeesa? You are there as a representative for those who are underserved— and you are doing this for my glory."

It's not about who I'm with. It's about who I take with me when I go. God will tells me how I need to present myself and give me the words to say. I just have to keep to the basics of who I really am, as expressed in my faith.

There was another situation, in early 2023, when I was asked to apply to be on the board of directors for the National Association for Free and Charitable Clinics. Even though they approached me for the role, they didn't choose me. Instead, they wanted me to serve on one or two of their committees and reapply for the board in two years. I couldn't help but question what was wrong with me and why they didn't pick me. Then, about three months later, Peace Health, a not-for-profit healthcare system with medical centers, critical access hospitals, and medical clinics in Oregon, Washington, and Alaska, asked me to become one of their system board members. I said "yes" because I had previously worked for them. As of this writing, I am the only woman and African American on their board, and I have the privilege of serving and traveling to any of their 17 locations in those three states when needed.

When God closes a door, He usually has something better that He wants you to do. I'm learning so much from Peace Health and their leadership. The experience is helping me to see people not by their diagnosis, but for who they are. The woman in the organization, a nun, told me, "I saw something in you that you didn't see in yourself. Don't go just where you are tolerated. I need you to go where you are appreciated. I appreciate you and what you bring to the table." That is allowing me to better appreciate myself.

Other situations have taught me the value of praising others, particularly those who are in authority over me. The chair of our board of directors is a doctor. I often tell him, "You are doing a great job. I enjoy working with you." That's how I show him I trust and appreciate him. I also collaborate with him on projects and initiatives at the medical center. As we work together, I am careful to let him know what he is teaching me in the process. I can just envision Lydia taking time as a merchant and a new believer in God to share her appreciation with Paul, Silas, and Timothy as she learned from them.

I want to be a person like Lydia because she knew who she was and what she was called to do. She trusted in it. In my life, I need to get past waning back and forth. I say I trust and have faith, but I can trip up. I have to learn to stand up, remember my integrity, and let God place my feet back on solid ground. When my integrity is not recognized or rewarded for whatever reason, I cry at first—but then I ask God to help me. Sooner or later (usually sooner), He shows me how that happened for a reason. Sometimes I think it is a test so that He can show me that integrity has its place even when others don't see it or respect it.

I am also learning to glorify God and give Him the praise more often than I have in the past. If someone at church says that I gave a wonderful message from the pulpit, I am going to praise God. If they tell me I look great, I say, "Praise God. It wasn't me. I didn't even want to get up today." Along with Lydia, I count my friend and mentor, Dr. Amanda H. Goodson, as a hero of the faith. When she asked me in October 2022 to go to Tucson, Arizona and speak on a panel at her church about operating in your spiritual gifts and exercising your anointing, she didn't know me from Adam. I spoke about boldness, and it was the best time I'd had in my life. It showed me I had something to give to others, and not just the ones who come into my church community every Sunday. It also let me see that someone else saw me. I admire Dr. Goodson for her walk with the Lord as well as her walk in her secular life.

I've learned that people don't care about what I say as much as they care about what I do. The old adage that actions speak louder than words is quite true. When patients come in the door at Volunteers in Medicine Clinic, I call them train wrecks because they have diabetes, high blood pressure, and other severe health care needs but no health insurance to cover the care they desperately need. As I take their eligibility information, some of them are loaded for bear, expecting me to tell them they don't qualify to be seen at the clinic. Then I say, "Yes, you are approved to be a patient here at Volunteers in Medicine. Let's set up your first appointment!" The look on their faces gives me such joy! They get to receive care, and it's free!

Sometimes, we are so used to being told "no" that we don't look at what God is doing—and I see God in the middle of my "yes" to these patients. I am an extension of God reaching down from Heaven to them and saying, "Yes, you can come to the table. Yes, we have room in the inn for you." Just being able to say "yes" gives me that oomph, knowing I am giving the acceptance—and hope. I love hope!

If we can simply give somebody hope, God will do the rest.

The best advice I've ever received came from Sister Monica Heeran, a no-nonsense kind of woman who was once the chief executive officer of Sacred Heart Medical

Center in Eugene and also a part of Peace Health Medical Center. Now 94 years old, Sister Monica once told me, "It doesn't matter whether I think you can do it or not. It matters if *you* think you can do it." In 2014, a decade after she said that to me, I had an *aha* moment when the economy tanked and the health care industry was up in arms. As a non-profit organization, Volunteers in Medicine is reliant on donations, and we weren't sure how we were going to get people to continue to fund us. Everyone was under the misconception that everybody was getting insurance from the federal government and would no longer need anything else. But there is a difference between just getting insurance and having insurance that will sustain you. A lot of people were going into the health insurance exchange and getting catastrophic insurance, not understanding that they couldn't use it unless they were hospitalized. They didn't know any better.

I joined the then-chairperson of the board of directors of the Coordinated Care Organizations, and we went to see their chief operating officer at that time, Terry Coplin. "You have all of these people out there receiving insurance," I said, "but you forget there aren't enough doctors out there for all of them to have access. If we took 300 of your clients and offered free health care services to them, would you give us a grant to help fund Volunteers in Medicine?" They agreed—and that sustained the non-profit for the next couple of years.

Thinking outside of the box like that has showed me that God is not a box stuffer. That idea was something that never would have come to my mind. It was not me. It was the hand of God. He simply used me as a vessel to deliver and execute it—and to prove the validity of Sister Monica's declaration to me.

As a woman of faith in the marketplace, the best opportunities I've had to excel and expand God's Kingdom have come when I speak the truth in love (Ephesians 4:15). We can allow people to think they are doing the right thing and keep the mask on their face, but when we tell the truth in love, they can then take the mask off and be who they are truly called to be. A lot of the women I have worked with as pastor in my church have told me, "Well, I come to church. I pay my tithes. I do this. I do that." But they don't always *love*. I had to tell one lady, "You come to church. You give lip service. You give work service. How about giving God service?"

She looked at me, and I thought she was going to cuss me out. Then tears started streaming down her face. "Does it show?"

"Does what show?" I asked.

"That I'm a fraud."

I leaned close to her and smiled. "You are not a fraud. I am giving you God's words and telling you what He wants you to hear. God loves you, and it's time to love yourself enough to trust that He loves you. When you trust that He loves you, it will allow you to love other people the way you should."

"I just don't understand," she admitted. "You don't know me that well."

"God does," I said.

That woman has become someone I can depend on. Even more, when I ask her to do something, she first says, "Let me pray about it," instead of, "Okay, I'll do that," and I know she is *truly* praying about it.

God is not a myth. He is the real deal. There are times

we need to be honest with ourselves and say, "I am the myth. I am the one perpetrating the fraud." We need to get to know Him for who He is—and I am called to help people get to know God for who He is on a level they have never experienced before.

If *I* can simply give somebody hope, God will do the rest. That's my measure of success. My actions may not have made everybody happy, but I did them while giving glory to God and obeying His voice. I want to hear God say, "Well done, DeLeesa, good and faithful servant. You did what I asked you to do today."

With that in mind, my faith strategy in the market-place is not to just go along with the crowd, but to use my spiritual discernment to see the situation as it truly is and respond accordingly. Likewise, we have to look beyond the situation and see where God is *in* it. We may not see Him right at that moment, but as we pray on all things and ask Him to reveal Himself, He will.

As I finished writing this chapter, one of my mentors told me that God has granted me favor with white people. At first I thought, *What? That's the stupidest thing I've ever heard.* But as I look back over the years, I see that I have sat at many tables where I would never have had the opportunity apart from God's favor. Little Huntington, Arkansas was where I started my journey, straddling the color line and finding my way. But I had to go from there to get to where God wanted me to be—and become who He has called me to be.

To give back.

To give hope.

Rev. DeLeesa Meashintubby is the proud pastor of St. Mark Christian Methodist Episcopal Church in Eugene, Oregon, the oldest African American church in Eugene. She is a wife, a mother of three, and a grandmother of one. She is also the executive director of the Volunteers In Medicine Clinic in Springfield, Oregon. She holds a degree in healthcare administration and several medical certifications. She also serves on the Board of Trustees of Bushnell University, PeaceHealth Board of Directors, and the Eugene Chamber of Commerce Board. In 2019, she was named the Eugene Chamber Business Leader Woman of the Year, and in January 2023 was awarded the Eugene Chamber First Citizen Award.

Contact DeLeesa at Dmeashintubby12@gmail.com

9

Keep Moving Those Mountains

Dr. Yvette Rice

Priscilla

"Greet Priscilla and Aquila, my co-workers in Christ Jesus."

(Romans 16:13, NIV)

"If you have faith (a firm relying trust) and do not doubt, you will not only do what has been done to the fig tree, but even if you say to this mountain, Be taken up and cast into the sea, it will be done."

(Matthew 21:21, AMPC)

Those words, attributed to Jesus Christ as He was speaking to His disciples, are inspiring to me—and provide a principle of hope for all women in the marketplace who face mountains related to gender and racial biases, as well as equal pay for equal work, daily.

According to McKinsey & Company In their comprehensive study, "Women in the Workplace 2022," women are "demanding more from work, and they're leaving their companies in unprecedented numbers to get it. Women leaders are switching jobs at the highest rates we've ever seen—and at higher rates than men in leadership. That could have serious implications for companies. Women are already significantly underrepresented in leadership. For years, fewer women have risen through the ranks because of the 'broken rung' at the first step up to management. Now, companies are struggling to hold onto the relatively few women leaders they have. And all of these dynamics are even more pronounced for women of color."[1]

In my book, *Mountain Moving Made Easy*, I shared about the mountains we face in our lives. The word "mountain," as used in the earlier Bible passage, is derived from the Greek word *ŏrŏs* meaning "proverbially, of overcoming difficulties, or accomplishing great things." I wrote, "Overcoming those obstacles or mountains in our lives does not depend upon our own merit or ability, but on whether we operate in the faith apportioned to us by God."

Thus, every day of my life, I must depend upon the Lord as I pursue my purpose in life—that includes my roles in the marketplace, previously as an engineer, and today as a corporate leader, minister, and business owner. I have dealt with gender and racial biases that brought me to my knees. As I did, I began to realize that my faith in

God was more about my life outside the walls of a worship center than inside. There were times I knew I had to wake up early in the morning, spend time with God in prayer, and study His Word to build up my faith, just so I could go into the office that day where I knew the mountains would be waiting for me.

In *Mountain Moving Made Easy*, I came up with an assessment of what faith means in our daily lives, describing it as being "an absolute, immoveable trust in God and His Word. We have to be strong in confidence that whatever the Lord proclaims through His Word, it is so! God's Word is the final authority for every situation in our lives. Simply stated, faith is living by absolute trust in God and His unchangeable Word." So, even when I feel led to operate in the gifts of the Holy Spirit (1 Corinthians 12:8-10) while working in the marketplace, I act according to the faith that is apportioned to me. Romans 12:6-8 teaches, "Since we have gifts that differ according to the grace given to us, each of us is to use them accordingly: if [someone has the gift of] prophecy, [let him speak a new message from God to His people] in proportion to the faith possessed; if service, in the act of serving; or he who teaches, in the act of teaching; or he who encourages, in the act of encouragement; he who gives, with generosity; he who leads, with diligence; he who shows mercy [in caring for others], with cheerfulness." (AMP)

We meet Priscilla in the New Testament, and she resonates with me as a leader in the church and in the marketplace. Priscilla served with her husband, Aquila, and taught other leaders in the church with him. The Apostle Paul specifically named her in his list of fellow laborers in the Lord. In Romans 16:3-5, Paul went so far as to say that they risked their lives for him, and that he and all the members of the Gentile churches were grateful for them. Paul also pointed out that one of the churches met in their home.

Priscilla and her husband are also prominently mentioned in Acts 18:1-4. "After this Paul left Athens and went to Corinth. There he met a Jew named Aquila, a native of Pontus, who had recently come from Italy with his wife, Priscilla, because [the Roman Emperor] Claudius had issued an edict that all the Jews were to leave Rome. Paul went to see them, and because he was of the same trade, he stayed with them; and they worked together for they were tent-makers. And he reasoned and debated in the synagogue every Sabbath, trying to persuade Jews and Greeks." (AMP) That same chapter of the Bible later details how Priscilla and Aquila instructed Apollos, an eloquent and cultured man well versed in the Hebrew Scriptures and taught in the way of the Lord, explaining the full story of the life of Christ more accurately to him.

There is no doubt Priscilla and Aquila were used by God to keep moving the mountains in people's lives. Paul respected them as a ministry couple, and several times he called her name first before that of her husband. In today's vernacular, we would name Priscilla and Aquila co-pastors, "a husband-and-wife devil-stomping duo."

I relate well with Priscilla and her husband because of the ministry assignment the Lord has given to me and my husband, Bishop Sam Rice, as co-laborers and leaders of New Genesis Community Church in Alabama. In many different scenarios, the Lord has used us to train and develop Christian spiritual leaders through our church's school of ministry. We have also found great joy in serving other pastors by helping them to develop their own church leadership.

Yet it wasn't always that way for the two of us in ministry—and as I look at what Priscilla had to deal with as a woman in ministry with a church in her house, I recall how Paul taught that women should be quiet in church. But that instruction was not for all churches everywhere, as many tend to believe. There was specific confusion going on in the church at Corinth at the time. Paul had to create order, and he was talking directly to the church at Corinth. Biblically, women are not only allowed to minister within the Christian church, they are welcomed to do so.

Priscilla was an example of just that, and she was totally out of the box as a woman teacher and leader during that time. She also inspired me when, years ago, my husband told me, in no uncertain terms, "Maybe you can teach the women and the children. But you *cannot* preach from this pulpit."

Our first child, Sharné, was two years of age when Sam accepted God's call into the ministry as a pastor. At the same time, God started tugging on my heart to go into the ministry—but there was a problem. We were in a church denomination that did not approve of women being in ministry roles. I did not want to violate church precepts. I also wanted to submit to my husband as I felt the Bible taught. Yet the Lord would not stop, until one night I was in my living room praying and the peace of God just melted me.

I heard Him so clearly. He said, "You didn't choose me. I chose you." I knew then that no matter what my husband said or the people in my denomination thought, I had to do what God was telling me to do.

From that moment on, I started getting invitations to speak at women's conferences. I was not ordained, but that didn't matter. I went and spoke, the fire of God hit me, and the power of God fell. I was so elated—until I came home. Somehow, word always got back to Sam, and for the next several days all I got were one-word answers to everything. "Yeah." "Uh huh." Looking back now, I know God was working on his heart, but I was miserable, and I told God I could not keep on living that way.

I had a literal walk-in closet that I used as my prayer closet, and I went in there on my knees and cried out to the Lord. "I can't do this!" I pled. "It is tearing my house apart. It is tearing up my family, and you do not call us to tear our family apart." I didn't realize it at the time, but God was using me to pull my husband out of his comfort zone.

I remember praying in my despair, "I just want to die, Lord. Just let me die." And I was dying. The Lord was crucifying me even while He was dealing with Sam. God showed me that it did not matter what I thought. He wanted to use me as a pioneer to open the door for other women, so I needed to die and get out of the way. From then on, if I was asked to preach or God told me to go somewhere to minister, I went and Sam dealt with it, usually in the same quiet way. Meanwhile, at the church itself, I took a back seat as much as I could and faithfully served him and the congregation.

A couple of years passed. Then Sam preached a message one Sunday morning out of the book of Matthew about how Jesus told Peter to get out of the boat. When he was finished, he announced to the congregation, "There is somebody here today, and God is calling you into the ministry. You are afraid to get out of the boat, but God's telling you to get out of the boat."

To this day, I don't remember how I got to the altar, but I went. Sam could have fainted. When he gave that invitation, he was surely expecting one of the guys, a deacon or someone else, to respond. Yet there I was.

When we got home, I asked him if he was shocked.

"Yeah, but when I saw you stand, I knew God said it was you."

A little while after that, God woke Sam in the middle of the night and took him from Genesis to Revelation, showing him every instance where He used a woman in the Bible. By the time I woke up the next morning, my husband was already awake, so I just got up, got dressed, and we went to church. He told me he wanted me to sit in the front row, and I said I would.

Before he began preaching, he told everyone in the church, "I need to do something." Then he looked right at me. "Yvette, would you stand up?" Adrenaline surged through me, and I hoped I wasn't going to collapse right there on the spot.

Guess what my husband did? He publicly apologized to me—and then he revealed how God has taken him through His Word and showed him every time He had used a woman. "Who was I to tell God who He can or cannot use?" Sam said. "God can use anybody. I have been wrong all of these years."

Within a month, we had two other women ministers that joined me in that congregation. Sam and I stayed there for another year-and-a-half before starting New Genesis Community Church, where we continue to be used of God—as husband and wife, man and woman—today.

As women of faith in the marketplace, there will always be times when our faith is pressure tested. When I was first studying engineering at the University of Alabama, I felt I had earned and deserved the opportunity to be there as an engineering student, but I did not yet fully understand that I was a female going into a field that was predominantly male, nor did I yet recognize the limitations I had because of what I had not been allowed to do previously. In high school, girls took home economics as an elective while boys took machine shop. That's just how it was. Therefore, when I got to college, the male engineering students had already been doing drawings and drafting, but I had never penciled a single mechanical sketch. My all-girls dorm provided tutors and study groups to make it easier for us to adjust to the engineering field, but it was difficult for me to learn to see things in a three-dimensional way because of my lack of drafting experience.

I was discouraged—until the day one of my engineering professors, a white man, brazenly told me, "You may as well go and change your major because you will never be an engineer. You are not going to make it." It was eye opening to me that a man, any man, would try to tell me what I was or was not going to do. I had never failed at anything in my life, and I was not about to start now. I buckled down, and within two years, I was in the civil engineering department specializing in petroleum engineering. I don't recall there being any black male students in the petroleum department, and some of the white male students befriended me and helped me. They saw my capabilities, and they considered me to be a fellow student, not a black female.

After I got my degree, however, the oil industry plummeted. Even the top students in my class were not getting job offers. Over the next year, the rejection letters came fast and furious in the mailbox, and at one point I thought I would never be an engineer. Then came the day my sister and I took her sons to the zoo. We ran into a black female engineer who had graduated with me who said she had gone back to school, took some mechanical engineering courses, and got hired right away. That was all I needed to hear. I signed up for a mechanical engineering class at the University of Alabama in Huntsville. Later, one of my mechanical engineering classmates told me his employer, Redstone Arsenal, was looking for female engineers. I filled out an application, and I was called in for an interview a few days later.

The woman who interviewed me said, "I'm sending you to this place first. If you don't like them, just come back here. I have another place for you to go. But before you leave here today, you will have a job."

So, I got my first job at Redstone Arsenal as a mechanical engineer in the structural engineering group, developing missile systems and light composite prototypes for different organizations. I was widely accepted by my peers—except for one older white male technician who clearly was not ready for *any* women engineers, regardless of their race. When I did my first real design concept, I drew it up and turned it in to him. He didn't really look at it, but got out his pencil, marked it up, and stated, "We are not going to use this." Despite my disappointment, I returned to my desk, meticulously removed all his markings, cleaned it up, and put it in the drawer. *This won't ever be used,* I thought, *but it's mine. It is my first work as a paid engineer.*

Then, less than a week later, the project office announced it wanted to use the design that matched up with my concept! The group did not know it had been marked up by the engineering technician. I pulled the drawing out of my storage desk and haughtily walked over to him. I'll never forgot the look on his face when I slammed it down on his desk and walked out. That changed his opinion of me, in part because I never told anyone what he had done, but also because he saw that I was not going to be intimidated by him or anyone else. He and I eventually collaborated on a couple of projects.

I worked at Redstone Arsenal for 10 years before another pressure testing moment came with my decision to take a 15-year hiatus from my career in order to raise our children, during which time I also wrote *Mountain Moving Made Easy* and helped to start New Genesis Community Church with my husband. Not only did that choice take faith for me, but it also stretched Sam's faith to support me. Just like Priscilla had in Aquila, God gave me a husband who walks in faith and welcomes the gifts God placed inside of me for use in the church, home, or marketplace. I was making twice as much as Sam at the time, and because I worked for the government, my health insurance coverage included dental and vision for our family. But I knew in my heart I was supposed to be home with our children. I had been traveling a lot, and I felt divided.

I remember the Lord distinctly telling me that I would be able to leave my job after our son, Chris, was born. God even promised me a date for the change: September 1. When I went to my supervisor, I wasn't sure what was going to happen. It was late August, and I was supposed to give a full two weeks' notice. Yet when I told him that

I was being led by God to leave work and become a full-time mom, he understood. He was a family man, he said, adding that his wife had made the same decision. He also told me not to worry about the notice, and that my last day would be, you guessed it, September 1. My supervisor's care and God's fulfillment of His promise superseded anything my mind could comprehend. Sam and I acted in faith, and God moved on our behalf. The state gave Sam, who was a probation officer at the time, a raise and added the insurance coverage we needed. It was incredible! We don't have to be afraid when God tells us to do something. He makes provision for all things in His time.

Finally, my faith was pressure tested yet again when, right after Chris' fifteenth birthday, God told me to get my professional resume ready. He wanted me to return to the workforce. I didn't. I thought, *You've got to be kidding me. Why? I'm content. I'm happy.* There was also the fact that I believed I could not return to my career as an engineer because of the amount of training I'd need to make up for the 15-year gap since I'd last worked. Sure, I had developed leadership skills training with my husband, teaching others how to become leaders, and I had been ministering in and through our church, all while taking care of our household. But I didn't know what to place on my resume. When I asked the Lord what to do, He simply answered, "Your skills." I had never heard of a "skills resume" before, but that's what I wrote as God led me. I didn't put in any dates. I just listed and described my skills and abilities and how they would play out in the marketplace.

Well, sure enough, the Lord opened the doors—and I was hired as a program manager for a government contractor for the United States Army Corps of Engineers.

My job was to teach others how to use the Corp's computer processing system. It was a very complex system, and I had been out of the technology field for 15 years, but they expected me to come in running because the contract was in trouble. I knew I had to depend on the Lord to help me and my team, so I got up early every morning to pray, spend time with God, and get a scripture for the day before going into the office.

It wasn't easy. Not only was I a woman running a team with members who weren't sure they wanted to be led by a woman in the first place, but the former leader of that team was now under my supervision. The software was built in-house and was new to me. Whenever an update or change was made to the system, we had to learn it and master it so we could teach it. There were days that the Holy Spirit would quicken me and say, "There is something wrong with the documentation here." I'd then go to my team members and ask them to look at it, and when they found the issue or problem I identified, they'd be amazed. They knew I was just learning the system myself. I relied totally on the gifts of the Spirit that God gave me, and I discovered that the gifts He'd given me were as much for use in the marketplace as they were in church ministry.

I felt just like Priscilla. She operated in faith, knowing that when God called her to do something, there was nothing in her circumstances that could stop her. I stayed with that company for almost eight years. I was blessed with bonuses and accolades. My team went from falling short of our clients' expectations to becoming 100 percent effective. I had faith that because God sent me there with an assignment, He would give me everything, including His grace, to get it done.

When I think of how my faith is inspired and equipped by the Holy Spirit, John 14:16-17 perfectly communicates the ways God helps me when I pray, study God's Word, and rely on Him. In it, Jesus says, "And I will ask the Father, and He will give you another Helper (Comforter, Advocate, Intercessor—Counselor, Strengthener, Standby), to be with you forever—the Spirit of Truth, whom the world cannot receive [and take to its heart] because it does not see Him or know Him, but you know Him because He (the Holy Spirit) remains with you continually and will be in you." (AMP)

My faith is comforted by the fact that the Spirit, who the world "cannot receive" is mine because I know Him, and He knows me. My faith is empowered as the Spirit advocates for me and uses me to be an advocate for other women. When I meet people, I often think I'm doing so for one reason, but God sees a totally different purpose to it. We have to be open and listen, even when we feel like the situation is impossible and we don't know what to do, and God gives us what we need. When I first went into engineering, I had a very difficult supervisor. He would say things that were almost insulting to both me and my husband, and I just kept dealing with it. The difficulty of the situation made me grow and look at my work and responsibilities differently. Over time, the same supervisor praised me in a functional meeting, bragging about the work I was doing. I didn't wish anything bad on this gentleman, and God ultimately moved me out of the situation. Throughout it all, my faith developed as the Spirit was my *advocate*.

My faith is deepened as the Spirit intercedes for me. There are times when I don't know what to pray for, but

He does, and He guides me. As my counselor, the Spirit informs my faith. I don't always know the answers, so if I have heard God and read the Bible, but I am seeking confirmation, God will send a business associate, a mentor, or someone else to confirm what He has been speaking to me and from whom I can seek and receive wise counsel. Men and women who live true to God's Word and follow His principles to develop their business are invaluable to me. The Spirit also counsels me on God's plans and strategies for my life and business as I pray silently or out loud for myself or for others. Scripture teaches, "Rejoice always and delight in your faith; be unceasing and persistent in prayer; in every situation [no matter what the circumstances] be thankful and continually give thanks to God; for this is the will of God for you in Christ Jesus." (1 Thessalonians 5:16-18, AMP) I don't just start my day with prayer and leave it at that. I have learned that prayer must be continuous throughout the day.

The Spirit strengthens my faith in much the same way He did for Priscilla. There was controversy within the early Christian church about the roles of women, yet Priscilla and her husband rose above it. I'm sure there were days of discouragement, and I imagine there were other times when people didn't want to hear them. Yet Priscilla and her husband literally risked their lives to fulfill their purpose (Romans 16:3-4). It's not accidental that Priscilla's name, in the original Latin, is *Prisca*, meaning "ancient and venerable." In the Webster's Dictionary, the word venerable speaks of someone who has earned "a great deal of respect especially because of age, wisdom, or character." She operated in wisdom as the Spirit strengthened her.

Finally, the Spirit infuses my faith as my standby, meaning that He is standing right there with me in whatever circumstance I am facing. I feel His presence, and I know when He is leading me and guiding me in the marketplace. He was doing so even as I started a new project in 2023 called Five Minutes to Victory where I encourage women online every Monday for five minutes. "Five" is significant: biblically speaking, it is the number for grace—and I certainly relied on God's grace to sustain my faith in 2020 when the COVID-19 pandemic hit. I had successfully started my own company by then, but the realities of social distancing resulted in my clients deciding to change or cancel their contracts with me because I could no longer see or interact with them as I had been.

I was scared, and doubt seeped in. *Hello, God,* I thought. *I made this decision for you. I started my business. What is going on?* In addition, my mother was severely ill, and I was caregiving for her, as well as helping Sam with the church. It was overwhelming. Then I heard God clearly say, "Oh, so you are the woman who wrote about mountain moving faith, but you want me to move the mountains." It was a statement, not a question, and I instantly realized that my faith was dwindling because I was not studying the Word enough. Romans 10:17 declares that "faith comes from hearing [what is told], and what is heard comes by the [preaching of the] message concerning Christ." (AMP) That's how our minds and souls get fed.

As the pandemic raged on, I entered into a renewed time of growing my faith and building my resilience by listening to the voice of God and moving forward. In Acts 1:8, Jesus told His disciples that the Holy Spirit would empower them to be His witnesses well beyond Jerusalem "even to the ends of the earth," (AMP), and that's what God did with me. Just as the disciples were pushed out of their geographical comfort zone, God used the pandemic to push me out of mine. I gutted my living and dining room and turned it into an office. I began using tools such as social media and videoconferences to create new content to engage my clients and opportunities to meet with them. I had to move beyond my camera-shy self and adapt to new ways of communicating. I discovered how to be comfortable teaching and consulting virtually—and my business not only recovered, but it expanded. Suddenly, I was being introduced to people that I would never have come into contact with otherwise because I sought God and let Him stretch me. God says He'll send us to the highways and byways, and when I think about it, the internet is truly the superhighway that has broadened my marketplace to people and places all over the United States.

———————

When I started my business management consultant company, LLVE, LLC (Ladies Living in Victory and Excellence), in 2015, I stepped out in faith. I attended a leadership conference where I had been asked to serve as the emcee. I set up a vendor table right next to the one for Strayer University. They were promoting a master's degree program in business from the Jack Welch Management Institute. I looked at the sign and thought to myself, *Lord, I need that MBA.* I already had a degree in engineering and a master's and a doctorate in theology, but I knew I needed a master's in business administration. I was teaching leadership and certified as a John Maxwell leadership trainer, but as a woman in the marketplace, I needed more credentials. In my heart, I sensed God was taking me further.

I talked to the sales team and found out the cost for the program: $40,000. There was no way I could afford it. But two years later, God sent another messenger who mentored and prayed with me. He told me, "God will take you further than what you have. You need more."

I was listening, but I didn't think anything else about it until a year after that when Strayer University opened a kiosk location for students in downtown Decatur. I saw it as divine intervention, especially after I learned Strayer was going to give away 50 scholarships, and I was contacted about it because I was on a particular board of directors. Strayer was looking for minorities to apply for the scholarships.

That was a wow from God! It was a total set up by Him! I applied, was awarded one of the scholarships, and was 59 years of age when I started the program. It took me three years, during which the pandemic hit and my mother's health deteriorated. There were times I worked through the night until two or three o'clock in the morning.

During one of my classes, I told the professor that I felt I had so much on me. I was trying to run my business, helping my husband at church, and dealing with my mother's constant care. I believed I had to drop the class.

"You cannot," the professor replied without hesitation. "You have a 4.0 in this class. You keep doing what you are doing, and I will work with you."

I knew there was purpose behind it, and I couldn't give up. Not only did I get through that class, but I got through all of them—and I graduated Strayer University with my degree and a 4.0 grade point average in 2021!

God answered my prayer! I didn't know that the storms would come in the middle of it all, but those only grew my faith even more because I had to rely on the Lord every day.

I still do as I employ my faith strategy as a woman of faith in the marketplace to daily hear and seek God's voice and direction. In 2022, God told me that I needed to rebrand some things for LLVE, LLC. In one sense, it was like starting over, but then I realized I was just continuing with a more strategic path. When I started the company, my tag line was "learning to live in victory and excellence." God said, "My desire is for you to focus on women because of the gaps in the marketplace." With that, I now focus on how living in victory and excellence is paramount for personal and professional growth for women in the marketplace in a continuously changing world. I tell women to do three vital things: 1) discover resilience, 2) build your confidence, and 3) become your best self. It was amazing how things started turning very quickly once I started doing what God said. He has opened one door after another, allowing me to fulfill my passion to add value to the lives of other women through developmental systems that promote discovering, building, and becoming a woman of excellence—and it's no wonder. The McKinsey & Company study I cited earlier was updated in 2023 to show that, while women are more ambitious than ever and workplace flexibility is fueling them, progress for women of color is still lagging behind their peers.

There is much work to do.

Now, every morning, I get up with a plan for what God wants me to accomplish more than what I want to achieve. There are times when I have a list of all the things I want to get done, only to have the Lord throw a wrench in my plans to get me aligned with *His* plans. Someone may have a greater need, or an opportunity may come that I wasn't anticipating. I don't own LLVE, LLC. God is the chief executive officer. I'm the chief operating officer under Him. I listen to His voice as He guides me.

As I look back at all the things I have been through over the years, I think of Romans 8:28, which tells us that all things work together for the good of those who love the Lord and are called according to His purpose. Whether as the pastor of a church, a leader in the marketplace, or as a parent or grandparent, everything, the good and the bad, culminate and work together for my good.

Operate in the faith apportioned to you by God—and all things will work together for *your* good as you keep moving those mountains in your life, to His glory!

As the President of LLVE, LLC (Ladies Living in Victory and Excellence), **Dr. Yvette Rice** is passionate about adding value to women's lives through developmental systems that promote excellence in the marketplace. Rice's focus on empowerment for women includes helping them discover resilience, build confidence, and become their best selves as women ready to successfully cross the gender divides of the marketplace and beyond.

A published author, Rice utilizes more than 35 years of expertise, influence, and business insight to partner with senior executives of large corporations to produce books related to leadership development, mentorship, executive coaching, and business advancement. Rice's mission as a keynote speaker is to feed the audience's faith and starve their doubts, inspiring them to act to fulfill their life purposes.

Contact Yvette at Yvette.Rice@LLVE-LLC.COM or www.LLVE-LLC.com

Notes

1   McKinsey & Company. "Women in the Workplace 2022," October 18, 2022, https://www.mckinsey.com/featured-insights/diversity-and-inclusion/women-in-the-workplace.

Conclusion

Lean Forward

These stories will equip and empower you wherever you may be right now. For self-reflection, what woman in the Bible did you resonate with you most and why? Perhaps it was one of our amazing co-authors who vulnerably shared the trials that have now turned into godly victories.

To recap, we heard from Odetta Scott, who shared Sarah, the mother of the Hebrew nation, and how you can follow His plan, not yours. Dr. Amanda H. Goodson introduced you to the life of Leah in Genesis 29-33 to show you how the impossible is indeed possible for you.

Elisa Marchetti (Lisa) journeyed back in time to the life of Deborah in Judges 4-5 to discern the "Five Cs of Faith" that are relevant for you today. The story of Ruth came to life through Je're Harmon, who inspired you with how you can respond to your life's circumstances so that every single thing belongs to Him.

Esther and Dr. Nannette Wright dove into encouragement so that you can let His light shine through you. Kim Dudley featured Mary, the mother of Jesus, and described how she persevered and pressed forward to advance the Kingdom of God in her society.

We saw the unwavering faith of Mary Magdalene and Rev. Yolanda Jackson, and Rev. DeLeesa Meashintubby introduced you to New Testament merchant Lydia to provide lessons and insights on how you can have a life of giving back and giving hope.

Finally, talk about moving mountains! Dr. Yvette Rice took you to the book of Acts and the impactful life of Priscilla.

We are here to remind you that God is not done writing *your* story. He is the author of your life, and we leave you with three truths from the Lord:

1. **God has given you favor.** In Genesis 1:27-28, it says, "So God created mankind in his own image, in the image of God he created them; male and female he created them." (NIV) You are uniquely created by God, and the creator deeply loves you.

2. **God has made you a bringer of life.** Isaiah 54:1-2 shows us how we bring vitality to the world. Have you ever thought of it that way? You are a vital leader who brings forth vitality! Whether you are a biological mother or nurturer of others, this is a competitive advantage It is not to be ashamed of, but instead shows your unrelenting strength and growth.

3. **God has created you to shine!** Isaiah 54:12 proclaims, "I will make your battlements of rubies, your gates of sparkling jewels, and all your walls of precious stones." (NIV).

Now it is your turn! Choose a woman in the Bible or one of the co-authors here to minister to you as you lead forward. It's time to make a difference now! You never know how one day your story will help the next generation of Women Leading by Faith!

Selah.